Reality Bytes Back

Bible character studies for young people including discussion questions and further reading pointers

Julian Hamilton
foreword by Andy Hickford

Kevin Mayhew

First published in 1999 by
KEVIN MAYHEW LTD
Buxhall
Stowmarket
Suffolk IP14 3DJ

0 1 2 3 4 5 6 7 8 9

ISBN 1 84003 345 2
Catalogue No 1500264

Cover designed by Jaquetta Sergeant
Typesetting by Richard Weaver
Edited by Elisabeth Bates
Printed and bound in Great Britain

Contents

Acknowledgements

T here are of course a lot of people who have helped me in learning about my Bible, and they are far too numerous to mention. In respect of this book there are a lot of people who have helped by way of encouragement, suggestion and ideas – thank you. I don't wish to draw people out in a special way but there are a few who deserve a mention. My patient, wise, and somehow always cheerful editor, Liz, with Kevin Mayhew Publishers – well done and thank you. The ever-present and effervescent staff here in the DYCW who continually entertain and encourage – thanks. The wonderful colleagues in life based at number 22 – let it roll on, and thanks. My friends in the west who read the manuscript and found the silly mistakes – from the south and the west, get ready, and thank you. My family, as always, who still manage to give me that fine balance of encouragement and outright loving banter that hopefully keeps my feet on the ground, and it is to my big sisters and brother that this small book is dedicated.

Lastly and firstly, to the one who knows everything and smiles at our attempts to do the same, eternal thanks and honour.

Foreword

The irrepressible Julian Hamilton has done it again. *Reality Bytes Back* is another devotional collection of Bible readings, personal reflections and prayers for the Christian reader.

This is sound-byte spirituality for the 21st century. Small helpings of deep truth in simple stories. It's easy reading and at the same time, hard hitting.

In *Reality Bytes Back* the story continues. Not the story of this book sequel, but the story that started back in the Garden of Eden and has continued throughout the generations as God has interacted with his people. *Reality Bytes Back* invites us into this story, to live out a new chapter – God's story unfolding through our own lives as we walk with him.

Take time to read. Take time to reflect. Take time to pray, and most of all, take time to go on living out the story of God's love for people, for it is in us that HIStory continues.

ANDY HICKFORD

Introduction

One recent survey said that less than 3 per cent of Christians in the UK read their Bible every day. I'm one of the 97 per cent. Another survey a couple of years ago by UCCF discovered that seven out of ten college students who have been heavily involved in their Scripture Union (Christian Union or whatever it's called), a number of years after college do not profess to owning a Christian faith. I'm glad I'm in the three out of ten who do, but I didn't go to the Scripture Union when I was in college.

This book is not an attempt to be radical and bring the Bible back to people, it is not an attempt to be scholarly (I'm not capable of that), it's not even an attempt to get young Christians reading the Bible every day.

What it is, is a collection of thoughts that arise from reading and meditating on different parts of the wonderful thing we Christians call the Bible. There is a lot for all of us within the pages of the Bible. Stories of pain, struggle, victory, failure, highs, lows, questions and security. We read about God, about his dealings with his people, and we read about ourselves. No matter what age we are, we know what it's like to feel bursts of excitement, but we also know what it's like to feel that our world may well come crashing down at any moment. God's words to us are complete and healing; we should dive into them and discover about ourselves as we discover about him.

Go ahead and meditate on it. What does that mean?

Quite simply, this is not a book that you will learn a lot from, although I hope you will learn some new things. It is not a book to just go into and grab a prayer, although if you can at times use it for that then that's OK. But primarily it is a book to help you be quiet. To help your mind settle and click into what God might be speaking into your life. The things written here are a culmination of thoughts over a long period of time – you may want to read a passage and think about it for days, you may want to work quickly. However you use the book, use it as you think and pray. Invite God to teach you as you become still. Take space and time out. Read it in your home, be quiet in your room, go for a walk beside the sea, take a stroll in a field, sit in your favourite coffee shop. But invite God to speak into your life. That is what it means to meditate on God's word. Dive into it and raise a generation who recognise that knowing the Bible is something exciting and meaningful which is an integral part of daily life.

There are a few ways in which this book differs from the last couple in the series. Most notably, there are sections at the end of each chapter that have questions and a few follow-up passages:

GO ON ⫸ heads the section of questions.

KEEP GOING ⫸ heads the section of Bible passages which look at themes raised in the chapter.

These are designed to help you if you want to keep things going in your own mind, or more probably, help a small group to keep discussion going. The questions are not all 'nice and easy, there is a right answer' type questions. They will stretch you . . . hopefully.

Gideon

I remember going on a school Scripture Union house party at the end of first form. It was an event that helped shape much of what I would go through in the following years. We were young and by the end of the week we were gasping for more of Jesus. We also had a great week climbing trees and chasing the girls, but that's another story. The reason I mention this is because I remember that we studied Gideon in the mornings throughout that week. We did it in small groups, we discussed the issues and we heard about this great army commander who delivered his people from their enemies. I don't recall too much more from those days – it was several years ago after all. (OK, fifteen!) But years later I have come back to the story of Gideon in the book of Judges and found out some things that I wasn't told about – for whatever reason – I suppose the teachers have their logic somewhere. But what is going on in this story is the triumph of an Almighty God who is able to use the weakest links in the chain to bring about huge victories. That's why it appeals to me now!

Day 1

Once again the people of Israel sinned against the Lord, so he let the people of Midian rule them for seven years. The Midianites were stronger than Israel, and the people of Israel hid from them in caves and other safe places in the hills. . . . Then the Lord's angel came to the village of Ophrah and sat under the oak tree that belonged to Joash, a man of the clan of Abiezer. His son Gideon was threshing some wheat secretly in a winepress, so that the Midianites would not see him. The Lord's angel appeared to him there and said, 'The Lord is with you, brave and mighty man!'

Judges 6:1-2, 11-12

Quite a dramatic calling, don't you think? These were days of trouble in the land for Israel. They were having their crops and livelihoods taken away by the Midianites, they were having to more or less hide in the hills because they could not settle anywhere else, and they were probably a bit annoyed about this . . . wouldn't you be?

But all is OK, because God is once again going to hear the cry of his people and send someone to help them (this has already happened several times in the earlier chapters of Judges). Only this time the choice is almost laughable. Gideon is threshing wheat – hiding in a hole while he was doing it – which was the least important job in the family. Later on we read that Gideon's clan is the weakest in Manasseh (Gideon's tribe – who by the way, earlier in the book were one of the tribes who failed to win battles for land in Canaan) and Gideon adds in verse 15 that he is the weakest in his family. So do you get the picture? Gideon is doing the least important job any member of his family had to do, doing it in hiding so that the grain he was threshing would not be stolen, and he is doing it in the family that are the least important in their tribe. And the angel comes along and says, 'The Lord is with you, brave and mighty man.'

Yeah, right.

But that's the thing about God . . . he sees a lot of things that we don't, and he knows a lot more than we do. Think just for a minute about how you feel about yourself – do you like you? What changes would you make? What do you think God would tell an angel to say to you?

The last thing Gideon would have expected to be addressed as was 'brave and mighty man.' Maybe God would address you as something you don't expect. Maybe he would just quietly say, 'I love you.'

Lord,
> you are a God of surprises,
> and I think that's cool.
> You see a lot more in us than we do,
> you see the promise fulfilled . . .
> Wow, that sets me up a bit,
> I feel like there is something to aim towards,
> something that you can do in me,
> something that you will say to me.
> Help me to know what you think of me,
> what I can do for you,
> what your big plan may be, how you can use me.
> And I suppose if you could use Gideon,
> maybe I can be of use to you, Father.
> Let it be,
> Amen.

Day 2 ....

Gideon replied, 'If you are pleased with me, give me some proof that you really are the Lord. Please do not leave until I bring you an offering of food.' He said, 'I will stay until you come back.' . . . . Gideon then realised that it was the Lord's angel he had seen, and he said in terror, 'Sovereign Lord! I have seen your angel face to face!' But the Lord said to him, 'Peace. Don't be afraid. You will not die.' . . . That night the Lord told Gideon, 'Take your father's bull and another bull seven years old, tear down your father's altar

to Baal, and cut down the symbol of the goddess Asherah,
which is beside it. Build a well-constructed altar to the Lord
your God on top of this mound. Then take the second bull
and burn it whole as an offering, using for firewood the
symbol of Asherah you have cut down.' . . . He was too
afraid of his family and the people of the town to do it by
day, so he did it at night.

Judges 6:17-18, 22-23, 25-27

If you have ever needed a bit of convincing about something, then you will understand how Gideon felt. All he
wanted was a bit of proof that this really was the Lord
doing business, and he got it . . . and he nearly wet himself
when he did. (In earlier parts of the Old Testament it was a
very dangerous thing to see the face of the Lord, and those
who were spared after doing it were always grateful, for
example, Hagar and Jacob in Genesis)

Gideon gets his assurance and is told to do something
that would have almost sounded worse than death – which
is why he did it at night! The Asherah pole was the pole of
the goddess of fertility, so any damage to that could mean
real problems for the people regarding 'ripe harvests' in
many ways; and by being told to destroy the altar to Baal,
Gideon is going to the very centre of what is going wrong
with this society. They had forgotten the Lord their God,
they were mixing with people who worshipped other gods
and the one true God hated it – it's in the commandments
after all. Gideon was going slap bang into the centre of
Canaanite religion and destroying it – good eh? Well nearly,
he did it at night so no one would see him!

However, it was still an important and brave thing to do.
And it is a thing that we need to do today without hesita-
tion. People have loads of things today that are more
important to them than God. The second family car, the big
holiday, the right investment to get more money, the drive
to be more popular than everyone else, the need to 'look'
right, the desire to get that one perfect partner can all

come before God. At the root of Canaanite society, and those who sympathised with it, was the worship of things that in the end wouldn't make a difference. Today we still worship things that will not in the end make a difference – except by making us more greedy.

What false altars can you try and destroy around you? What false altars can you destroy in yourself?

Lord God,
    it must have been frustrating at times
    working with Gideon.
    Did it upset you that he did this thing at night . . .
    or were you just glad he did it?
    I suppose you were happy that he did get it done,
    and helped promote your holy name.
    I want to do that, Lord,
    I want to look and see where things are
    that people see as more important than you,
    and I want to help destroy them.
    Not just so that I can be destructive,
    but so that I can help build something better,
    in your name.
    It sounds like a big task, and I suppose it is,
    but show me where to begin.
    Thanks.
    Amen.

Day 3...

Then they said to Joash, 'Bring your son out here, so that we can kill him! He tore down the altar to Baal and cut down the symbol of Asherah beside it.' But Joash said to all those who confronted him, 'Are you standing up for Baal? Are you defending him? Anyone who stands up for him will be killed by morning. If Baal is a god, let him defend himself; it is his altar that was torn down.'

Judges 6:30-31

Clever, don't you think? It's a great argument, and it's true. And what's more it worked – remember that people living in this time in these situations were not known for their temperament and fair sense of justice!

What really impresses me is that the defence comes from the family. Even though Gideon had caused a stir that could embarrass the clan, and maybe harm the family, they still let him in and stand by him, while daddy sorts it out. Reading this passage makes me really aware of how serious the state of the family is today. It's not what it should be. And I am only too aware that according to the law of averages many people reading this will have an experience of family that only conjures up pain and anger, and maybe a great deal of hurt.

I count myself very fortunate, that when the chips are down and the heat is on, my family would do anything and everything to help. They have shown that in the past, time and time again. That does not mean I don't annoy them, or at times they don't annoy me. It does not mean that there isn't anything about me they wouldn't change or make better (there have been times when I've been told in no uncertain terms the kind of clothes I should be wearing!). It does mean that I have a safe house, a place of acceptance, a place where I am welcomed and forgiven because I am me and they know me. Gideon felt that in the above passage. We all need that.

For some, these words will just bring tears because you have no family. Some might feel guilty about how you treat your family, and others will be able to relate to my experience and realise how fortunate you are.

Two things. This generation needs to fight to regain the family – it is a battle, and it's a difficult one. But past generations have let us down and we have a God-given duty to try and fix what has gone before. And we need to start treating each other as family. There are too many people who do not have the faintest idea what 'family' may mean – we are all God's children, and we need to start living out what being part of that family means.

Lord Jesus,
  you came and loved everybody,
  you treated everyone as special.
  I want to pray for the people who are closest to me,
  those who look out for me,
  those I call my family . . .
  Hear my prayer.
  Amen.

Day 4

Then Gideon said to God, 'You say that you have decided to use me to rescue Israel. Well, I am putting some wool on the ground where we thresh the wheat. If in the morning there is dew only on the wool but not on the ground, then I will know that you are going to use me to rescue Israel.' That is exactly what happened. When Gideon got up early the next morning, he squeezed the wool and wrung enough dew out of it to fill a bowl with water. Then Gideon said to God, 'Don't be angry with me; let me speak just once more. Please let me make one more test with the wool. This time let the wool be dry, and the ground be wet.' That night God did that very thing. The next morning the wool was dry, but the ground was wet with dew.

Judges 6:36-40

You might have thought Gideon was getting the message, until all these goings on in the above verses took place. He had seen the angel of the Lord, he had seen the offering which he gave spontaneously combust, and he had destroyed the altar to Baal in the village, building an altar to God in it's place – and got away with it (with a little help from the family!). All good powerful displays of God's power and God's control over the situation. And still Gideon acts like a chicken and has God up two nights in a row moving fleeces!

The thing is, I know I've done the same kind of exercise. I have been in places where I have clearly seen the work of God. I have had times in my life when I have felt God standing right beside me. I have listened to the witness of

16

people who tell me in an amazing and powerful way what God has done in their lives. And still at times I ask for something like a fleece. Still at times I ask God if he is really in control. Still at times I ask God is he listening at all.

At least Gideon has an excuse – God is telling him that he is going to deliver his people from their enemies! No wonder Gideon wanted to be sure.

God points out elsewhere in his book that it's OK to bring all our thoughts to him. And that's something I know I am doing on a regular basis. But I guess that deep down the thing that really bugs me about the above passage is that I'm simply jealous . . .

Lord,
>   you know my mind,
>   you know my heart,
>   and you still love me.
>   Thank you.
>   You know the struggles I have,
>   and you know the times
>   that I have asked for assurance.
>   Nothing as grand as a fleece job,
>   just something small, just to let me know
>   I'm doing the right thing.
>   Sorry for wanting the fleece at times,
>   and sorry for being jealous of Gideon
>   who did actually get it.
>   Work with me, Lord,
>   please send your assurance at different times,
>   just so I do know I'm OK with you.
>   Thanks.
>   Amen.

Day 5..

The Lord said to Gideon, 'The men you have are too many for me to give them victory over the Midianites. . . . Announce to the people, "Anyone who is afraid should go back home, and we will stay here at Mount Gilead".' So twenty-two thousand went back, but ten thousand stayed. Then the Lord said to Gideon, 'You still have too many men.' . . . Gideon took the men down to the water, and the Lord said to him, 'Separate everyone who laps up the water with his tongue like a dog, from everyone who gets down on his knees to drink.' There were three hundred men who scooped up the water in their hands and lapped it; all the others got down on their knees to drink. The Lord said to Gideon, 'I will rescue you and give you victory over the Midianites with the three hundred men who lapped the water. Tell everyone else to go home.'

Judges 7:2-7

Do you get the feeling that God is really trying to say something through this story of Gideon? I really do . . . and here is another key moment. Gideon is finally ready to go into battle for the Lord – after all the assurance, checks and balances he could get his hands on. He is as sure as he is going to be – and even that's not too sure. Can you imagine the face of Gideon as God is telling him to keep losing men!

Firstly, a simple request, 'Anyone who is afraid should go back home.' And he loses two thirds of his men. And to be honest, I don't think that being scared is a reason to duck out of battle – especially the battle of life. Take the example of Burmese democracy leader An Sung Shu Chi, who as a little girl was scared of the dark, so she got up in the middle of the night and walked around her house until she was bored!

Then comes the water thing. Follow this – if Gideon was going to use the brightest and best men, do you not think that he would have chosen those who knelt to drink? They would have still been alert and ready to get up quickly if attacked. Not like those who lapped the water . . . their heads would have been practically in the water! But those three hundred are the ones God says he is going to use.

The whole story so far boils down to this: God has taken the least likely person, from the most unlikely place, given him the least likely proof for his task, and resourced him with the most unlikely set of soldiers for battle. God wants to win this battle on his own merits, not the merits of man.

How often do we remember God in what is going on around us? We are good at pointing out all that is wrong, we are great at calling for the evil to be banished from society, and we are excellent at special events to let people know how to fix this world. None of us do anything on our own. God is behind it – he is behind our very existence. Of course God hurts when he looks at his world, but he also provides ways ahead, and we have to remember that they are God's ways, not our ways.

Lord,
    I find it hard to remember sometimes
    that you are at the heart of everything.
    That what hurts people in this world, hurts you.
    That you are calling people to you,
    and that will make things better –
    when we all do your work here.
    Thanks for caring so much,
    and for using different ways to heal this place.
    I pray, Lord, that the glory will be yours,
    people will know that you are working today,
    and you alone deserve the credit.
    Thanks, Lord, you're the best.
    Amen.

Day 6 ....

Gideon and his hundred men came to the edge of the camp a short while before midnight, just after the guard had been changed. Then they blew the trumpets and broke the jars they were holding, and the two other groups did the same. They all held torches in their left hands, the trumpets in their right, and shouted, 'A sword for the Lord and for

Gideon!' Every man stood in his place round the camp, and the whole enemy army ran away yelling. While Gideon's men were blowing their trumpets, the Lord made the enemy troops attack each other with their swords.

Judges 7:19-22

Deep in the South Indian Delta, if you go walking around – looking out for tigers – you may see little lizards that look like fish with legs. They *are* fish with legs. In fact they are called sand lizards, and when the water level is high they swim like fish and live in the water, when the water level goes down they live and walk on the land. You may also see salamander lizards, lizards who live on the land, but who also swim when the water gets too high. I love these wee animals. They have adapted perfectly to their surroundings, and they have broken the normal rules of nature (fish don't walk on land, lizards don't swim) to be able to survive in the delta.

Gideon's tactics had to be adapted in the battle above. He had planned on having many men, now he only has three hundred. Previous to this, God had given him yet another proof of his victory by letting him overhear a dream that the enemy camp has had, which tells of the victory Gideon will have over them. (Dreams in those days were believed to be sent directly from God.) Gideon sees what he has, uses his intelligence, and in the end there is no fighting on the part of the Israelites, because the confusion makes the enemy attack each other.

It was not the way Gideon had planned the attack. They came, hiding their bright lights under clay pots, at the time of night when the guard had just been changed so the new guards would not be totally used to the darkness, and they created a lot of noise and a lot of light . . . it would have been frightening, particularly if you believed you were going to be beaten in the battle. Gideon has the victory for the Lord.

In today's world there are many battles that have to be fought for God. In homes where many people suffer; (one child a week dies in Britain due to violence or abuse) in society where big business keeps the gap between those who have and those who have nothing, growing; around the world where countries in the third world suffer because the western countries insist on collecting the debt they are owed; in our churches which have become dull and irrelevant, no longer showing a gospel of love and peace between God and man; and of course, in our lives where we need to make the difference ourselves. Are there places where we need to change tactics and move on to a winning formula for God?

Probably.

Lord God,
    you are powerful, and you care
    about the oppressed,
    and often this world doesn't.
    You are loving and you care for those who hurt,
    and too often we ignore them.
    Help us, Lord, to learn more about
    the battles you have for us,
    the battle you have for me.
    I know, Lord, there is so much to be done,
    and I know that the difference has to begin in me.
    I pray that it will, Lord.
    I pray that you would send your Spirit
    to guide my path,
    to show me where I should be doing battle.
    To give me the courage to be strong
    in your power
    and in what you can achieve.
    Use me, Lord,
    I am yours,
    here I am.
    Amen.

GO ON ≫→

1. How easy is it to think that God actually wants to say something to you? (Day 1)

   Do you think Gideon was expecting such a visit from God – and such a task? (Day 1)

2. Gideon reacted in a certain way – probably a way that most of us can relate to. Are there things you can do to invite God to speak to you, and make sure you are listening, or would you have reacted in the same way as Gideon? (Day 1)

3. Gideon was asked to go into the heart of where his culture and society had gone wrong. Where do you think God wants his people today to make the difference? How can we do it? (Day 2)

4. Gideon felt the protection of his family – are there times you can relate to where you have felt the same protection? (Day 3)

5. Are there times when you have clearly felt the support of your heavenly Father? (Day 3)

6. What steps can you, as a young person, take to help in the regaining of strength in a family unit? (Day 3)

7. In what ways do people today test God, and do Christians do it? (Day 4)

8. It may well be said that Gideon simply didn't have 'faith' that God would do what he said he would – do you think that's true? (Day 4)

9. What, if anything, does Gideon teach us about faith? (Day 4)

10. So God takes the most unlikely guy, from the most unlikely place, to do the biggest job of the day, with the most unlikely bunch of people – does that give you hope? Why? (Day 5)

11. Gideon fought and won a victory that he didn't want to fight, and thought he couldn't win until the last

minute. He did it by being ready to change his mind as to how to go into battle – we have a lot of people in our churches who are getting tired in battle, can you think of new ways God may want his people to engage in fighting for him? (Day 6)

12. The battle 'tools' that Gideon's men used are not what you could call conventional, what 'tools' do we as young Christians need to fight for God and for his Kingdom to come in the world where we live?

KEEP GOING »→

- Listening to God – 1 Samuel 3:1-21
- Family stuff – Luke 2:22-52; Genesis 25:19-34; Ephesians 5:21-6:4
- Battling for God – Ephesians 6:10-18; James 4:1-10
- Faith – Matthew 11:2-6; Daniel 3:7-18

Habakkuk

This guy is a minor prophet tucked away at the back of the Old Testament. I have discovered he has a remarkable amount to say about life today. As I have read the book I have been challenged by what Habakkuk saw and what I see as I look around. There is a lot of pain and suffering in what he sees . . . but he deals with it in the right way. He tells God about it. The name Habakkuk actually means 'wrestler' – ever seen those guys in the Worldwide Wrestling Federation? Well, he's not one of them. It means that he grappled with God on serious questions, he did not hold back from God on account that his queries and complaints were too difficult for God to handle, or too hurtful for God to be able to deal with. He comes out and talks about what is going on . . . we should do that.

It is also interesting that most scholars would place Habakkuk living around the 600BC mark, living and working around the Temple in Jerusalem. If this is a true and accurate account of the time of writing, everything that Habakkuk prophesied comes true in the years that immediately follow the book.

There is a lot more to Habakkuk than I am capable of bringing out in a few days of meditations . . . why not get into it a bit more if you find you have a taste for what the Lord is saying through these words.

Day 1 ....

O Lord, how long must I call for help before you listen, before you save us from violence? Why do you make me see such trouble? How can you endure to look on such wrong-doing? Destruction and violence are everywhere.

Habakkuk 1:2-3

It was about 11pm and it had been a normal, quiet night. Two friends had gone to the video store to get a video and had failed to make a decision – so I went and made a choice . . . and a fairly obscure one at that. It was almost finished and I was getting tired. Suddenly one of those moments happened. About seven gun shots rang out at the end of the terraced road where we lived.

We froze for a couple of seconds, then jumped to open the curtain, carefully, to see if anyone was running past. After a minute or two we ventured into the street, at the top of which was a police station. Police were running everywhere, the army arrived within two minutes and the familiar police tape used to cordon off a crime scene was wrapped around the lamp posts.

One body lay in the middle of the road and reports of other injuries in the restaurant at the top of the street began to circulate. I asked the inevitable questions of a couple of policemen there. Is he dead? Is it a policeman? Do you know who did it? As time passed it emerged it was not a paramilitary killing, it had been a drug killing – one man dead, one woman lying in hospital fighting for her life.

Over two and a half thousand years ago Habakkuk cried out to God about violence and having to look at bad things. Today we still have to do it. The angels must turn to God sometimes and ask, 'When will they learn?'

Lord,
    so much wrong goes on around us daily.
    It must cause your heart to break.
    I know it really gets to me at times.

I don't have any answers, Lord,
and that frustrates me.
I get angry at bad people and bad things.
Sometimes I hate them.
I don't think that's the right attitude,
but I need you to work with me on it.
I suppose if it hurts me, it really must hurt you,
because you love everyone.
I find that difficult, Lord,
I'm not sure how to love those I see leaving pain
as a trademark.
I need your help with that one too.
Help me, Jesus.
Help me to look beyond present suffering
to a bigger purpose.
In your holy name I pray.
Amen.

Day 2 ....

The law is weak and useless, and justice is never done. Evil men get the better of the righteous, and so justice is perverted.

Habakkuk 1:4

The papers are full of them these days – miscarriages of justice. People who spent years in prison for a crime they did not commit. Just yesterday an elderly woman walked out of prison after five years with the courts saying, 'Oops, it looks like we made a mistake and you did not actually kill your auntie – sorry!' Somehow I think a response of, 'Oh that's OK, I'll just nip home for a cup of tea now, thank you very much,' is difficult to imagine! When life is unfair it leaves a bitter taste. When I was at school I'm sure I got punished justly many times (OK, so I wasn't exactly an angel all the time). But the times I remember are the couple of times that I was unjustly punished . . . one dining hall potato-throwing incident will forever stay in my memory! It wasn't fair.

It's all around us now, as it was in the day of Habakkuk. The rich are still rich and the poor are staying poor. At the time of writing, one quarter of the world is living in abject poverty (that's poverty on the less than $1 a day standard), human rights are being trampled on in many parts of the world – military dictatorships oppress people in the Congo and Burma, to name a couple. And in the case of the UK, the present government gives less than 0.3 per cent of its GNP (all its money in simple terms) to the developing world – the United Nations recommended amount is 0.7 per cent. It's not fair.

I know if you thought about it you could come up with a lot of things in your life that aren't fair – I know I could as well. But try this for a while. Remember what we do have, what we have been given in comparison to many who do not have. An old friend of mine, years ago when I asked him why he was so happy, said to me, 'There's always somebody worse than me.' He was probably right . . .

Lord,
 There is so much injustice and suffering
 around this world,
 I know that it breaks your heart.
 I'm sorry for things which I do
 that help the unfairness to continue.
 Maybe if I tried to be fairer myself,
 it would make some small difference.
 Even in how I treat the people next to me,
 those across the road,
 those in school,
 those in work.
 I think that fairness in the world
 has to begin with me,
 can you help me deal with it, Lord?
 Help me to be strong
 and treat people equally and justly.

It sounds simple and yet I know it's not,
I know I need your strength to do it.
Please assure me that if I stick my neck out for justice
you will protect it . . .
Amen.

Day 3...

Keep watching the nations round you, and you will be astonished at what you see. I am going to do something that you will not believe when you hear about it.

Habakkuk 1:5

At this point I would have to confess that I am as sceptical as the next man . . . maybe even more so. I do spend a lot of time searching for the rational explanation for a particular miracle. I wonder about the state of mind of a person who has had something of a St Paul on the road to Damascus experience. I query in my head the validity of midnight visits from angels. And remembering that the most common first words an angel says when encountering someone in Scripture are 'Do not be afraid', I'm usually willing to take people at their word rather than ask for an angelic visitation myself!

It could all be that I am an outright unbeliever at times, it could be that God has given me an appetite for investigation. It may be that my faith isn't even up to the size of a mustard seed yet (heaven help me if I ever need to move a mountain). It could have something to do with being brought up in a home where the Christian faith was very much a practical action type thing, it may also have something to do with those great questions of faith . . . Why did that child die? Who is she to receive forgiveness? Why bother? What difference can one person make anyway?

I've studied psychology of religion, and religious conversion in particular, and so my queries may all focus on the need that people have to find God in their lives at a given juncture. Or maybe I still harbour somewhere in my deepest level, something of the insecurity and panic of being a teenager in the mid 1980s (stop laughing).

Maybe it could simply be that like Habakkuk, I don't believe it. More than anything, I want to see God's spirit poured out in a way that makes people fall to their knees. I've been asking for that for a while now. Maybe I still don't believe it. Have you been asking for that? Have you been asking for anything? Do you believe it?

Lord,
> forgive my over-indulgence.
> My thoughts of worry and questions.
> I know you have given me the ability
> to think and question,
> and I'm grateful . . . usually!
> I pray that you can help me deal with the things
> I don't believe,
> not to gain a rational explanation,
> or a clever theory,
> but a living faith.
> One that trusts,
> because it can't see,
> and doesn't understand.
> May the glory be yours when the mighty things
> happen in this land.
> Amen.

Day 4

I am bringing the Babylonians to power, those fierce, restless people. They are marching out across the world to conquer other lands. They spread fear and terror, and in their pride they are a law to themselves. . . . They sweep on like the wind and are gone, these men whose power is their god.'

Habakkuk 1:6-7, 11

I find this passage intimidating and a bit scary. With most of the passages I find intimidating and scary, I move on and leave them to some kind of scholarly bloke/chic. Alas there was no escaping this one . . . in terms of Habakkuk, it's fairly important to get a hold of.

You may recall Habakkuk has been listing all that is wrong with his land at the time he is living in. There is a lot of suffering, a lot of pain, and a lot of turmoil. What God says is almost too easy an answer, but it's what God says. And he says it loud and clear in the above passage. Here we read that all that happens, happens under God's sovereign rule. He is in control. Ultimately . . . the earth is the Lord's and everything in it. Comforting? Good. It gives me comfort too. It tells me that in the pain and suffering of the world there is meaning – we may not see it yet, but there is purpose. If we suffer, just for suffering's sake, then there is no purpose, there is no reason. If God is in control then there is reason, there is purpose.

There is another very important thing in the above passage. The Babylonians had taken the liberty they had been given in being vessels of God's work too far (by the way do you find it interesting that tribes outside the 'chosen one' can be messengers of God's divine plan – I find it fascinating!). Later on in the book (most of chapter two) we read that they pay for going too far with the 'lead' God had given them.

God does allow us freedom, indeed God has provided a way for us to be totally free (the cross of Jesus), but at times the freedom pitch can be a very dangerous one for those of us who continually make bad decisions. The Babylonians found that out to their cost. I'm still learning that.

Lord God,
    I thank you that you are in control.
    It gives me hope.
    It helps me feel secure.
    Help me to live all day, every day remembering it.

I think I must give you some fairly difficult situations
to deal with!
Thank you for never leaving and saying,
'Sort this one out yourself!'
I pray that I will not take liberties with the freedom
you give to me,
but that I can feel free to be the person
you made me to be,
totally and utterly yours.
Amen.

Day 5 ....

*I will climb my watch-tower and wait to see what the Lord
will tell me to say and what answer he will give to my
complaint.*

Habakkuk 2:1

I was fifteen (I think) and I was with twelve other Irish
teenagers, in a forest in Germany, camping with about
twenty German teenagers. Boy we had some fun. We
went to groovy water sport places, we walked around the
forest, we had great water fights, we walked around the
forest, we got to know each other really well.

One of the most memorable things about that camp was
the flagpole. A flagpole with a flag that we were told the
lads from the local village would try and steal one night. As
a consequence, we each had 'watch duty'. Every night,
from midnight to 2am and from 2 to 4am two of the team
had to guard the camp.

At 3.30am on the morning I had the late shift with one
other Irish bloke, I had a memorable experience. It was
drizzling with rain, the trees swayed in the shadows and
the forest was at its blackest moment. You never were sure
exactly what was going on behind the leaves. As we were
coming towards the end of our shift (and as my blood
pressure was coming down) an owl twit-twooed, and
scared the living daylights out of me. When I had changed

33

my pants, I thought about how close I had been to waking the entire campsite screaming, 'It's them, it's the Germans, they're here, get up and defend the flag.' (Maybe not the most diplomatic of stunts I have ever pulled.) It would probably have meant a serious kicking.

Being on watch, and being patient is not as easy as it sounds. I found it difficult in Germany that summer. I find it harder at times when I'm trying to wait on God to see what he will do in a given situation. I get frustrated, annoyed and anxious that God is not dealing with all that goes on around this land and this world. But I live in time: God is outside it. I know a bit: God knows all.

Full marks to Habakkuk for coming up tops in this area . . . he says he will be patient and see what the Lord will do. We should try the same.

Lord,
    I know in my heart that you are in control,
    it just takes a while to work it into everyday practice.
    Those people who are seen
    as spiritual giants around me
    are people who seem to get this right,
    they can wait upon you,
    and have tremendous grace about it.
    I'd like that, Jesus,
    I'd like to be able to be content to wait patiently
    and watch your will unfold,
    and enfold all around.
    Help me to practise a bit of grace, Lord,
    for your glory.
    Amen.

Day 6 ....

O Lord, I have heard of what you have done, and I am filled with awe. Now do again in our times the great deeds you used to do. Be merciful even when you are angry. . . . I will still be joyful and be glad, because the Lord God is my saviour. The Sovereign Lord gives me strength. He makes me sure-footed as a deer, and keeps me safe on the mountains.

Habakkuk 3:1-2, 18-19

At the end of this book, even after everything that Habakkuk had complained and 'wrestled' with God about, we get to a real place of conclusion. At the end of the day he gives the glory and the praise to God, he acknowledges the mighty power and strength that comes from above. Here's how he gets there.

During the preceding verses Habakkuk has been 'praying' – a musical liturgy or song that Habakkuk would have been familiar with is the most likely source. In it he 'remembers' all that the Lord has done. The first half of chapter three talks in wonderful language about how the Lord became the master of the seas . . . this was a big thing for Hebrews; and the second half tells how the Lord has overcome his enemies. We therefore have the Lord being the total master of the whole of the created world – nature and humankind. There is nothing beyond or above him. Habakkuk sends out this praise and comes to the conclusion at the end of the book that the Lord is his strength.

Maybe it would be wise at times of wrestling to praise God and meet him there – after all 'God inhabits the praise of his people.' After coming to this conclusion of God being our strength, Habakkuk goes one step further and tells us in the last verse that God will equip us for whatever is ahead. Deer hooves are the most sure and steadfast footing for the mountains . . . that is the footing God will give his people. He will not just be present with us and be our strength, but he will enable us to meet whatever we come across on the road of life.

A good last word from Habakkuk? I think so.

Heavenly Lord,
>   you are mighty and powerful,
>   you have created everything,

all living things are under your control.
Thank you for the assurance
that I'm part of that living order.
I treasure being part of your creation
and I love that you look after me.
I would like to call on your strength
a bit more often, Lord.
To feel your mighty arms around and about me,
your warmth, your care, your power.
In times of trouble you will be my leaning post
and I will lean on you.
Thank you for being a great and powerful God,
interested in helping me.
All the honour and power belong to you,
now and for ever.
Amen.

GO ON ⟫→

1. Have you had an experience where all you have been able to do was ask, 'Why Lord?' (Day 1)

2. How did God come to you in that time? (Day 2)

3. How did you change, if at all, through that time? (Day 3)

4. It's not a fair world – what does God want us to do about it?

5. Do your church and your community do things to bring about justice in the world? How can you help if they do, how can you start them if they don't?

6. There are a lot of questions raised on Day 3 of this chapter. Do you think there are times when honest questioning is a good thing to do? How do you think God responds to our questions?

7. What experience do you have of having your questions answered? (Day 3)

8. What areas of belief do you struggle with? Have you given those areas in honesty to God? (Day 3)

9. When all around is going daft, the Bible teaches that God is in control. Where can you see it to be true? (Day 4)

10. God has given freedom to his people – freedom to mess up and go too far. When, or where do you think people today have gone too far? (Day 4)

11. Was it fair of God to make us as people who have the freedom to mess things up? (Day 4)

12. 'Being patient and waiting on God.' What does that mean to you? (Day 5)

13. How can we learn to take time to be quiet before God, and how can we teach a world that is going ever faster about patience? (Day 5)

14. Can you think of situations in the past where you have felt the strength that God gives, working through you – a time when you knew you were not walking the road of life by yourself? How did you feel at that time, and what did you learn about yourself, and about God?

15. Habakkuk says God will equip his people. What equipment do you feel you need at the moment? Have you asked God to provide it – or more to the point, have you asked God to provide the equipment that he knows you need?

KEEP GOING ⟫→

- Pain and heartache in the world – Lamentations 5; Psalm 22

- Justice for this world – Isaiah 58:6-10; Matthew 20:16

- The strength of God – Joshua 1:6-9; Isaiah 40:12-31; John 17:6-23

Jonah

. . . .

This is one of 'those' stories. I learnt it, and I think a lot of other people did, at Sunday school. And I always got all the questions right as well. Why? Because it was a classic 'silly' story. Thus demonstrating the brilliant biblical truth, that the more far-fetched the story the easier it is to remember! It was also easier to learn because, let's face it, there was always a rather bizarre interest in how on earth someone could survive, covered in fish guts!

The Bible contains many different kinds of writing – poetry, songs, historical account, story, prayer, and so on, and now that I have left the ranks of the Sunday school I am looking at this story in a different way . . . a way that helps me hugely where I live today. There are people who take every word the Bible says as having literally happened – that means every single word is for real: history, poetry, story, parable, etc. That's a valid position to hold if it helps you in your faith (difficult though it is for me to sustain – 'the eyes of the Lord range throughout the earth' 2 Chronicles 16:9 . . . look out for the heavenly eyeballs!) In this piece of writing it seems that the writer is trying to do more than just give a story about a guy called Jonah. If we go along this path of enquiry, then we can presume that God is trying to teach us something important – and we should always listen when that is happening.

If we take Jonah to represent certain pious Jews who thought no one except themselves should get God's favour, and Nineveh to be a people that these hard-line Jews did not care for, then the story opens up for us into today's world. Given the humour and irony that the writer uses, I think it would be safe for us to walk down this path.

Go on and read the whole book now before reading on – it's not very long, it's easy to read . . . and it's near the end of the Old Testament.

Day 1 ....

One day, the Lord spoke to Jonah son of Amittai. He said, 'Go to Nineveh, that great city, and speak out against it; I am aware how wicked its people are.' Jonah, however, set out in the opposite direction in order to get away from the Lord.

Jonah 1:1-3

I would not do this now, but I did it then! It was a really nice summer evening in my home town of Bangor, and I was walking to a cafe called 'The Boulevard'. This was a shop that a local church had taken over and was running as a drop-in centre. It was a great project, but the terms of the lease meant that they were not allowed to 'preach' as such. That worked well because the kind of people that were coming in did not want to be preached at in any way. There was another local church, a very strict and 'fundamentalist' small denomination, who most nights would hold an open-air service about five feet away from the front of the building . . . thus putting some people off who would otherwise have come in.

This particular evening I took exception. I decided I would do something. So I walked out the back door and went to the pavement opposite where I knew there would be people giving out tracts. As planned, one of the young guys stepped out and gave me a tract (must have thought I needed it), at which I stopped and asked him, 'What makes you want to give me this?' He went white! But within two minutes the other people giving out tracts had closed in and we were soon having a huge theological fight. Within five minutes the open-air service had stopped and those involved in it had crossed over the road to us, by which time the other people in the drop-in cafe had come across the road as well and everyone was hard at it! I jest not when I say that the police turned up.

Thinking back, it may have been that I was doing what Jonah did in the start of this book. We do not read that

Jonah fled because he was afraid of the Lord, or because he thought he was not up to the task, we are simply told that he ran to get away from God. It could have been because God had told him to go to Nineveh. These were people that Jonah would have felt were not worth it, the people Jonah did not think God should show mercy to. Jonah felt God was being unreasonable. In other words it was not a matter of fear, it was a matter of theology. Jonah thought he knew better theology than God.

When we think we know better theology than God we end up having theological fights on seafronts because we cannot let God do the talking.

Lord,
    I know that there are times
    when I feel I'm on top of things.
    Times I am sure I'm listening to you.
    Times I'm sure I'm doing the right thing.
    I pray, Lord, that I will think about you more
    in my decisions,
    and what it is you want me do.
    It can be hard at times to listen to you,
    especially when others disagree
    with what I think you are telling me.
    Maybe you could give me courage to be strong,
    to be sure about doing your will,
    and not think that I know best.
    Maybe then I can gain some real insight
    about what your will for my life is.
    Thanks.
    Amen.

Day 2..

But the Lord sent a strong wind on the sea, and the storm was so violent that the ship was in danger of breaking up. The sailors were terrified and cried out for help, each one to his own god. Then in order to lessen the danger, they threw the cargo overboard. Meanwhile Jonah had gone below and was lying in the ship's hold, sound asleep. The captain found him lying there and said to him, 'What are you doing asleep? Get up and pray to your god for help. Maybe he will feel sorry for us and spare our lives.'

Jonah 1:4-6

Remember what I said about humour? This is a classic example of a great moment from Jonah's life. Just picture it – all around is going crazy, the waves are coming over the side, the sailors are running around throwing stuff overboard, the wind is howling, everything is as frenzied and furious as it could be, and there's Jonah . . . 'Zzzz, zzzz, zzzz, zzzz!'

I want to draw your attention to a great piece of irony here. (Check out Alanis Morrissette's definition in *Isn't it ironic* for a good hint on what it is.) Jonah is the holy boy who God wants to use to do his will, the 'chosen' one to take the good news to the people of Nineveh, and yet it's the sailors who are being religious. They are praying as hard as they can to get themselves out of trouble. We know that they are praying with a totally limited understanding of who God is (because each prayed to his own god), but at least they did it! And what's more they give us a good lesson on prayer, because after they did it, or probably even as they are still doing it, they are taking action to get their prayer answered – throwing cargo over the side! That's the best way to pray . . . action is as big a part of prayer as the words are. Also it's the captain who alerts Jonah to his religious duty to pray. The heathen tells the godly man how to behave in a godly way!

When I was younger I thought God only spoke to a certain kind of person. A religious 'churchy' person. I think I did the Kingdom a lot of damage by being presumptuous. Things like, people who didn't go to Scripture Union in school could not possibly have a faith, or thinking I had all the answers on what exactly a daily Christian walk was. It happens all around us today – those who feel unwelcome in Church because of how they look, people who feel the need to have the same Bible translation as everybody else, people who only look for God's hands where they have already seen them. We limit God when we do that. I hope God gives me the chance to make some amends for those days.

It's really worth remembering this is all born out of the theology that God is chasing Jonah to harm him – that's why they are all so scared. Pity the sailors couldn't read on in the story the way we can. God is only coming after Jonah to turn him around.

Almighty Father,
    thanks for the truth
    that not only do you love everybody,
    but you can use everybody, too.
    It's pretty weird to think of it,
    because that gives you ultimate control,
    and I think that scares me a bit.
    But I pray that it will comfort me, inspire me,
    help me to feel even more yours.
    And I pray that I can stop
    being judgmental about others,
    because that's your job and not mine.
    There is so much for me to learn about others –
    and that's cool.
    I'm going to look for signs of you wherever I can
    from now on.
    Amen.

Day 3 ....

The sailors said to one another, 'Let's draw lots and find out who is to blame for getting us into this danger.' They did so and Jonah's name was drawn. So they said to him: 'Now then, tell us! Who is to blame for this? What are you doing here? What country do you come from? What is your nationality?' I am a Hebrew,' Jonah answered. 'I worship the Lord, the God of heaven, who made land and sea . . . Throw me into the sea, and it will calm down. I know this is my fault that you are caught in this violent storm.' . . .So they cried out to the Lord, '. . . Don't punish us with death for taking this man's life! You, O Lord, are responsible for this; it is your doing.' Then they picked Jonah up and threw him in the sea, and it calmed down at once. . . . At the Lord's command a large fish swallowed Jonah, and he was inside the fish for three days and nights.

Jonah 1:7-10, 12, 14-17

When I was at school I remember quite clearly people who made a definite decision not to be a Christian. We even had the setting up of an 'anti-God' squad at one point. I have a vivid memory of walking down the drive after school one day with a girl who had recently gone out with people the S.U. group (of which I was one) didn't think were suitable! She had done some foolish stuff, and now felt the need to renounce her faith – the emotional pressure some people from the S.U. put on her was seriously rough. We all made mistakes then: the girl, (doing 'bad' stuff) and those of us trying to 'win her back'. We had made conscious decisions and we were sticking to them – because we thought that's what God wanted. We thought we knew better than God did!

Since those days I have come across people who have made similar decisions in life. Jonah is making a decision in the boat. He is telling the sailors that it is all his fault. He is the cause of the trouble, and therefore it is he who must suffer. That's why he tells the sailors to throw him over the side. Once again Jonah knows best – so he thinks anyway. Thank God he intervenes on our behalf. Thank God he intervenes and shows us that even in our bad mistakes and errors of judgement we are still not beyond his reach.

Have you ever felt like it's all too difficult, or that you just can't make the grade? Take heart, Jonah thought he knew better than the Almighty and acted accordingly – and God still stepped in to help him.

Lord,

    it's good to know that you are on my side.
    I've done stuff I'm not proud of,
    and a lot of it I've brought to you.
    But there were some things
    I thought were better kept to me.
    I'm sorry for making that decision,
    there is nothing you don't know about anyway!
    I think it's excellent that you didn't just let Jonah
    get away here,
    but even in his mistakes you helped him.
    I pray that even in the mistakes that I make
    you'll help me as well.
    I belong to you.
    Amen.

Day 4 ....

'In my distress, O Lord, I called to you, and you answered me. From deep in the world of the dead, I cried for help and you heard me. . . . I went down to the very roots of the mountains, into the land whose gates lock shut forever. But you, O Lord my God, brought me back from the depths alive. . . . I will sing praises to you; I will offer you a sacrifice and do what I have promised. Salvation comes from the Lord!'

Jonah 2:2, 6, 9

Sometimes in life things change! One minute Jonah is taking his own decisions, deciding what God's punishment for him should be, the next minute he is sitting in the belly of a big fish lamenting God's kindness by saving him. A turnaround for the books, I say!

God has a habit of doing that. There are people who will tell you quite openly and honestly about how they reached the depths and felt they could go no further down, when God took hold of their lives and brought them up. That reassures me. It reminds me of the kind of God I have on my side.

The other things about these verses is that Jonah is saying words that can be found elsewhere in the Old Testament. They are things he would have learnt as a boy, things he knew from 'Sunday school' (although they didn't have it on Sunday and it wasn't a school!). They were basic teachings about God, and they were important for Jews . . . and they enabled Jonah to give voice to what he was feeling.

A while ago I was talking to a man who works with alcoholics. He talked about the fact that a lot of older alcoholics will express regret, remorse, and will say that they have let their family down; they used to go to church and now they have failed God as well. But with young people addicted to drugs and alcohol, there is little regret and remorse. They have not been brought up in Sunday school, they do not have the basics to go back to. Jonah was glad of his basics. And we need to learn what we can, whenever we can. You never know when you will be in the depths and what you may be able to go back to from days gone by.

Lord God,
    once again I read about you being patient and kind,
    about you stepping in and saving Jonah,
    about how Jonah was so grateful,
    and how he showed it.
    Was he really glad, Lord?
    Did he really know what you had done?
    Was he ready now to go on and do your work?
    I think there was a bit of him that was just glad
    not to be sitting at the bottom of the sea!
    And I think there are people now who say things
    they don't mean when you help them,
    I pray that I won't be one of them.
    Thank you for the words of Jonah.
    Thank you that you did save him,
    and I'm glad he was so grateful.

Maybe I should practise being more grateful
for the things you have done for me.
Here are some of the things I'm thankful for . . .
Yours is the glory for ever.
Amen.

Day 5 ....

*Jonah started through the city, and after walking a whole
day, he proclaimed, 'In forty days Nineveh will be
destroyed!' The people of Nineveh believed God's message.
So they decided that everyone should fast, and all the
people, from the greatest to the least, put on sackcloth to
show that they had repented. When the King of Nineveh
heard about it, he got up from his throne, took off his robe,
put on sackcloth, and sat down in ashes.*

Jonah 3:4-6

Talk about a reaction to God's word! It's what every
minister dreams of, it's the stuff books are written
on, it's a sure-fire repentance moment. And how did
Jonah help bring this about? Well, he walked into the city
and said in a loud, clear voice, 'Forty days, you're history.'
That was it. Nothing about the unconditional love of an
eternally forgiving Father who just wants his people to
acknowledge him as their creator and redeemer. Fire and
brimstone evangelism, you might say. And it worked! I said
in the introduction several pages ago about the irony and
humour in Jonah – here it is again. But the point is well
made don't you think?

Jonah's heart was still at home, he gave a little and the
little he gave he gave begrudgingly. Remember Jonah does
not think that the Ninevites deserve God's saving, hence
the proclamation of the word of God that basically said,
'There's no escape, you're ashes soon enough.'

But God is God, and God is good. He takes the little that
Jonah gives and turns it into an opportunity for good.
(Remember there is no movement of God without the Holy

Spirit.) God took little and made it big, God took just enough and made it huge, God took a small offering and made a saving act for the history books.

Do you think God could still do it? Why not ask?

Dear God,
> you've done it before
> and I believe you can do it again.
> Show your power today,
> make it count.
> Here is my offering of myself,
> I pray I can be used for your glory . . .
> Amen.

Day 6 ....

Jonah was very unhappy about this and became angry. . . . The Lord answered, 'What right have you to be angry?' . . . Then the Lord God made a plant grow up over Jonah to give him some shade, so that he would be more comfortable. . . . But at dawn the next day, at God's command, a worm attacked the plant, and it died. . . .[Jonah] wished he were dead . . . But God said to him, 'What right have you to be angry about the plant?' Jonah replied, 'I have every right to be angry – angry enough to die!' The Lord said to him, 'This plant grew up in one night and disappeared the next; you didn't do anything for it, and you didn't make it grow – yet you feel sorry for it! How much more, then, should I have pity on Nineveh, that great city. After all, it has more than 120,000 innocent children in it, as well as many animals!'

Jonah 4 . . . parts of. . . !

I received a letter from a friend several years ago. In it was a photocopy of a letter from a woman to the editor of a Scottish Christian magazine. In the previous issue there had obviously been a letter from a youth leader talking about how Jesus would communicate today with young people. The woman was not happy. She wrote about the 'usual rubbish from young people' in the letter she was replying to. She said that young people have no right to get on the way they do, and should follow the example of Jesus in how he respected the Church. (Which he did, but let's not forget that at one point his love and respect led him to call the ministers of the day hypocrites and snakes. Matthew 15:7; 23:33)

I have no doubt this woman meant well. I have no doubt that she felt she was doing the godly thing. But her basic problem is the same one that Jonah had a few thousand years ago. She, and he, could not take the grace and acceptance they had been shown by God and show it to others. Jonah had been saved from drowning, had been looked after even though he tried to run away, and in the above verses he was even given a plant to provide shade. Yet he was still unhappy about this kindness being shown to the people of Nineveh. God shows us his love in so many different ways – providing, looking after, giving direction, being tender, giving grace, comforting, guiding (to name a few ways), that we have no excuse for pretending we don't know how to pass it around.

We need to start doing that – remembering the grace that has come to us first.

Lord Jesus,
> I have received so much from you.
> Thank you.
> So often I just carry on regardless,
> forgetting all you have done.
> I don't show others the love you have shown to me.
> I don't give away as much as you have given to me . . .
> and I know I could never give away that much
> because you have given me everything,
> but that's not an excuse – I think I make it one.
> Forgive me for being unable to give more of myself
> to others,

and for thinking that there are people
you will not work with.
I am yours . . . help me remember that,
and then keep acting like one of yours.
Amen.

GO ON ⫸⫸→

1. Have you ever felt that you knew God better than
    someone you were having a 'debate' with? What was
    the outcome of the meeting – did you change, did
    they? (Day 1)

2. How can God use people who disagree for the good
    of his Kingdom . . . or can he? (Day 1)

3. Can you think of a time God spoke to you, or a person
    God spoke to you through, that surprised you? (Day
    2)

4. Think of people and places where you could show
    God's love – and where people may be surprised. (Day
    2)

5. Have you ever felt that you were running from God –
    and that God was chasing you with a heavenly iron
    rod? How do you feel to know that God was coming
    to Jonah to turn him around and not to harm him?
    (Day 2)

6. We all make mistakes in life – it's part of being human.
    Jonah felt that he needed to react to his mistakes in
    the way he had been taught he should, i.e., it was his
    fault, and so he must take the blame and act accord-
    ingly. How difficult do you find it to let go of things
    done in the past? God sends the big fish, even when
    the last thing Jonah thought would happen was that
    he would be saved by God. Do you find it difficult to
    believe God would love you in the same way? (Day 3)

7. Jonah was able to go back to things in the past and
    use what he had learnt. Can you think of people,

places, events, books, churches, that you are thankful for? What impact did these people, places, etc., have on your life? (Day 4)

8. How can you continue to do for others what these people, places and so on did for you? (Day 4)

9. Could you have told the people of Nineveh what Jonah told them? (Day 5)

10. Can you think of situations where you have avoided saying the hard thing? What were the consequences? (Day 5)

11. God takes the small things we offer and turns them into big things for his kingdom. What small things can you offer God? (Day 5)

12. Are there people that you find hard to love?

13. Jonah had to face a situation where people he felt did not deserve God's grace had received it abundantly – he didn't take it well, and God showed him that his love was open to everybody. Where are the people in your life, your community, your school that you may feel deep down don't deserve God's grace? How can you begin to allow God to use you to help them? (Day 6)

KEEP GOING ≫→

- Running from God – Luke 15:11-32; 2 Chronicles 28:1-6

- Letting God be God (and using us for his purpose); 1 Timothy 1:6-8; Colossians 2:6-15; Genesis 18:1-15

Joseph

I could only have been eight or nine – but the experience was one that will stay with me probably for the rest of my life. I used to do my own shows on the landing stairs, and get my long-suffering mum and dad to watch the show, which was usually a pantomime. I even had the sense to take the bedroom table lamps and turn them towards the upper landing – they were great spotlights. My parents laughed. If I were to see a video of those shows now, I would probably cry. But then came the real thing.

Our church decided to put on a version of the musical *'Joseph and the Amazing Technicolor Dreamcoat.'* It was my 'professional' stage show debut (aside from the children's afternoon talent show in Aberystwyth, Wales – but more about that another day), and it was sensational. I was one of the children in the chorus. I had to wear an all-in-one specially made frock thing, really fetching. But I loved it. I've never really been able to stay away from a stage since. Joseph was pretty good, Potiphar's wife was amazing, and Pharaoh rocked. Special.

For that reason, the story of Joseph has always had a special place in my heart – the music, the sound, the lights, the comedy, the colour – all of it intrigued me for years. Then almost twenty years later, I went back to it, to see if there was anything I missed – and well, yes, there was. The following meditations are only a few thoughts taken from a very long story.

Day 1 ....

One night Joseph had a dream, and when he told his broth-
ers about it, they hated him even more. He said, 'Listen to
the dream I had. We were all in the field tying up sheaves
of wheat, when my sheaf got up and stood up straight.
Yours formed a circle round mine and bowed down to it.'
'Do you think you are going to rule over us?' his brothers
asked. So they hated him even more because of his dreams
and because of what he said about them.

Genesis 37:5-8

When I was in the musical years ago, I thought Joseph was blameless. It was the big bad brothers who were the sole wrongdoers in the picture. But I must confess to thinking as I read the above verses, 'what a jerk'. I mean, what was Joseph thinking of? The brothers already hated him because they all knew that Joseph was Jacob's favourite. It is mentioned more than once in the biblical introduction, just so we get the picture . . . questions do have to be asked about the 'coat' thing!

Jacob, earlier in Genesis, had been involved in family strife . . . he had blackmailed his brother, and had stolen his father's blessing from him. And all spurred on by his mother who wished to see her favourite son above the son her husband favoured. That's putting it simply, but Genesis gets very complicated! And anyway, Jacob is put out by it all because he has to run away to escape his brother's revenge. Into all of this, add the fact that Jacob is then tricked into marrying the sister of the girl he really wants to marry, and has to wait seven years before he can marry who he really wants (Joseph's mother – and that at least explains why he is so fond of Joseph!).

I think we tend to come into biblical stories 'cold' a lot, but this background really helps me build a better picture of what was going on in Jacob's household. Maybe Joseph was being a bit tactless and insensitive by running and telling his brothers (and the whole family in the next verses) that he was going to rule over them – if your younger brother or sister said it to you, what would you say! But he is not alone in fault, Jacob has some questions to answer as well. (How did he think the brothers would react to Joseph with all the special attention?)

Jacob should have learnt a lot from his own experience of family trouble – he didn't. We all need, no matter what age we are, to constantly ask where we are and where we are going in life – and more importantly, what have we learnt? If we forget the lessons of today, tomorrow will be a lot worse.

Lord God,
    heavenly ruler,
    teacher,
    friend,
    thank you for being interested in my life,
    and for having a hope that I can make it better.
    I'm learning a lot as I get older,
    and I know there's a lot of it
    I really need to remember.
    Not my astro-physics or my Russian verb tables,
    but my lessons in life.
    My lessons on people,
    and how easy it is to hurt them,
    or how good it can be to go out of my way
    to make someone smile.
    Jesus,
    there are great things going on around me,
    please help me to always look to see
    where you are working.
    Amen.

Day 2

Judah said to his brothers, 'What will we gain by killing our brother and covering up the murder? Let's sell him to these Ishmaelites. Then we won't have to hurt him; after all he is our brother, our own flesh and blood.' His brothers agreed, and when some Midianite traders came by, the brothers pulled Joseph out of the well and sold him for twenty pieces of silver to the Ishmaelites, who took him to Egypt.

Genesis 37:26-28

Funny how some things change really quickly, don't you think? You may well have seen the film *Pretty Woman* starring Julia Roberts and Richard Gere, it was the 1980's at its best! In it there is a scene, where Julia, who played a Hollywood prostitute, has been asked by Richard Gere to spend a few days with him. So he gives her a lot of money and tells her to go shopping for some dinner dresses. She walks into one shop on the highly sophisticated Hollywood Boulevard, the ladies take one look at her, and ignore her. She has all this money to spend, but because of the way she looks they make her feel like rubbish. Richard Gere takes her back to the same shop the next day. He walks in and tells the store manager that he has a huge sum of money to be spent, but they will need some serious 'sucking up' to, and they get it – every assistant on the shop floor is running around in a frantic manner trying to please them. It is an amusing change, but it demonstrates a change brought about by greed.

That's what happened above. Judah has seen his elder brother Reuben tell everyone not to kill Joseph, and he now sees an opportunity for gain. He even uses the sickening words, 'after all he is our own flesh and blood'. Fairly amusing considering only a couple of verses before he was going to help kill Joseph. All it took to change his mind was the chance of a quick profit.

Who knows, maybe if Judah hadn't given them the idea they would have just given Joseph a bit of a going over and then taken him home? Maybe they would have left him there for a while, then come and got him? All we know is that one person's idea for a quick profit let the situation get an awful lot worse. And we know that the same thing has been happening down the centuries ever since.

Lord,
it's really sad to see that sort of thing going on
in biblical times,
I thought it was only nowadays
that people were really greedy.
I suppose that was wrong.
And I'm not even sure I know what I can do.
There are so many people just out to grab
what they can get,
all the adverts,
the posters,
the magazines,
it all seems so good at times, Lord,
just what I need!
But I know that's not really true,
because you are all I need.
And I suppose my prayer, Lord,
although it's quite hard to say,
is that I can remember to be true to you,
and your values.
I'll try and keep it fair, Lord,
not be greedy.
Give me the strength to know what I really need,
not what I think I need.
Amen.

Day 3 ....

Joseph was well-built and good-looking, and after a while his master's wife began to desire Joseph and asked him to go to bed with her. He refused and said to her, 'Look, my master does not have to concern himself with anything in the house, because I am here. He has put me in charge of everything he has. I have as much authority in this house as he has, and he has not kept back anything from me except you. How then could I do such an immoral thing and sin against God?' Although she asked Joseph day after day, he would not go to bed with her.

Genesis 39:7-10

It's good to know that Joseph was getting on well in Egypt! If there was a book written about making the best of a bad situation, I'm sure Joseph would figure. But that's not the main point of the above passage. You don't have to be a genius to see what is going on . . . Joseph – new boy – doing well – everything is under control. Rich man's wife – not satisfied with all she already has – 'Oh please, you know you want to' – Joseph in jail set up a stormer.

This will probably sound bad, but I'm really impressed with Joseph. I honestly don't know too many males who would have taken the stance that he did. Sure there was certain death if he had been found out, but there are an awful lot of people down the ages who have taken the risk.

It's the most basic temptation that we have – easy sex. The concept is sold in millions of homes around Europe every day. Magazines, television, and advertising to name a few, all exploit the basic human desire for sexual intimacy.

The way Joseph sets out his stall to resist her onslaughts I think is interesting. Several chapters earlier in Genesis, Joseph's great grandfather Abraham, had let people believe that his wife Sarah was his sister (the excuse is that it was done to protect them both!). As a consequence King Abimilech took her over to his place one night, but when he discovered the truth he prayed about the mistake, saying it was done in good faith – because he really didn't know that Sarah was married to Abraham . . . God agrees that it wasn't a sin. In the above passage, Joseph is in no doubt as to whom this woman is, and so what he says I think is important. He sees it as not just a sin against his earthly master who has given him great responsibilities, but more importantly he knows it is a sin against God. That's the line that Joseph took – 'Yes, it would be bad for me and you, but more importantly it involves God.'

Good for Joseph – OK, he ends up in jail totally set-up, but he is there with a clear conscience . . . God hasn't left him.

Lord God,
it's everywhere – even in the Bible!
I'm glad that Joseph stuck up for himself
and I think I know how hard it was.
Because if all humans are created equal,
then we all know how tempting it can be.
I pray, Lord,
that as I keep getting older,
you will keep teaching me more,
about intimacy,
about real love,
about how you want me to behave.
I know that when I mistreat others,
that hurts you.
And I know that when I mistreat myself,
that hurts you too.
Thanks for sticking with me, Lord.
Let me be all yours.
Amen.

Day 4 ....

The king said to him, 'I have had a dream, and no one can explain it. I have been told that you can interpret dreams.' Joseph answered, 'I cannot, Your Majesty, but God will give me a favourable interpretation.'

Genesis 41:15-16

My name is Julian, and I'm a Methodist. There, I said it. There are a lot of things that come with being a Methodist in today's Ireland – not least the fun of being a minority Protestant church, who do not subscribe to the works of Calvin, in a place where the majority are Calvinists!

But that's all too technical. Anyway, John Wesley is generally credited with being the founder of Methodism – although I like to think that it was God's idea. Many Methodists today look at the works and words of our founder for guidance and learning. Some of us also like the Bible! But with all of that (which, by the way, I think Wesley would agree with) he was by all accounts an incredible individual, with a passion for the gospel rarely seen nowadays in the church he established. The best sermon I have ever heard preached on John Wesley was delivered in Cliff College, England. And it wasn't delivered by a Methodist, but by an Anglican Evangelist – hmmm, interesting, considering that they chucked him out of the Anglican Church over 250 years ago!

Anyway, when the sermon was finished people began to applaud. And this rather getting-on-in-years gentleman simply looked up to the ceiling and pointed towards the heavens. It was a telling moment.

Joseph did the same thing several thousand years before that evangelist in England. The king asks him if it is true that he can do what he has been told he can do, Joseph replies, 'Not me, God.' And that was after being falsely accused and being thrown into jail.

It's a good lesson.

Jesus,
    I know I don't stick up for you enough,
    and I'm sorry.
    I know I'm not your greatest ambassador here,
    and I'm sorry for that too.
    I also know that when things are going well
    I don't give you the credit.
    Lord, I want to thank you for all you have given me,
    all I have and am,
    it's all from you.
    Thank you, Lord.
    Let it be now and for ever.
    Amen.

Day 5 ....

Judah went up to Joseph and said, 'Please sir, allow me to speak with you freely. Don't be angry with me; you are like

the king himself. . . . I pledged my life to my father for the
boy. I told him that if I did not bring the boy back to him, I
would bear the blame all my life. And now, sir, I will stay
here as your slave in place of the boy; let him go back with
his brothers. How can I go back to my father if the boy is
not with me? I cannot bear to see this disaster come upon
my father.'

Genesis 44:18, 32-34

O nce upon a time there was a family of chipmunks who lived in the forest at the bottom of the garden. One day while mummy was out shopping, little Jack, the eldest of the chipmunk brothers, decided he would be brave. You see, he had heard about the family of squirrels that lived across the ocean (it was really only a pond). His friends had told him about how the squirrels had arrived in the garden after the chipmunks, but it was they who had taken all the good grass, and what's more, there were a lot more of them, so they got all the bigger nuts. As daddy came back from work he saw little Jack begin his journey out of the safe-lands, he called to him to stop, but Jack pretended not to hear him. He was a big chipmunk now. After a very long journey, Jack saw a squirrel in the distance – hatred filled his little puffy cheeks. He lived in hiding for months watching the squirrels from afar, never going too close, planning how to exact revenge on these squirrels for being alive. He thought he had a good plan. He was going to target them one by one, because he noticed how they often went out alone to get nuts. All the while Jack's family got even more worried.

The day came when Jack was at the top of a huge chest-nut tree and he saw a squirrel pass beneath the branches – he took aim and let the biggest chestnut he could find fly out of his hand toward the unsuspecting squirrel below.

The last thing the squirrel saw before he woke up in squirrel hospital was a rather large chestnut land beside him, and a dark, furry chipmunk-shaped blob coming hurtling towards his head.

Soon after the accident had happened the other squirrels arrived and took both the casualties to hospital. And when Jack first woke up his first instinct was to get up and run because all he could see were squirrels! Unfortunately for him, he was too badly hurt to get up, and fortunately for the end of this story, he had to stay in hospital for a whole three days. This is good for the story because it was while he was there that he actually talked to some squirrels and more than that, discovered that there was no reason to hate them, indeed he made friends with some of them. After this had happened, the other chipmunks were only too glad to talk to the delegation of squirrels that helped Jack home. They came to tell the others what had happened, and to talk about co-operation in the garden. Jack led the talking for the chipmunks, and not too long after that, there was peace in the garden – the change was brilliant. In fact, if you were in the garden today, you would see the squirrels and chipmunks playing together. Lovely.

Think back to the start of Joseph's story – it was Judah who had the idea to sell him.

Lord,
> there are times when I don't believe it's possible
> to change.
> Times when I find it hard to think
> that people who have hurt me
> can change and be sorry.
> I suppose that's when it changes
> from being their problem
> to being mine.
> Jesus,
> help me always to remember your power
> that changes people.
> And let it change me.
> Amen.

Day 6 ....

Jacob packed up all he had and went to Beersheba, where he offered sacrifices to the God of his father Isaac. God spoke to him in a vision at night and called, 'Jacob, Jacob!' 'Yes, here I am,' he answered. 'I am God, the God of your father,' he said. 'Do not be afraid to go to Egypt; I will make your descendants a great nation there. I will go with you to Egypt, and I will bring your descendants back to this land. Joseph will be with you when you die.'

Genesis 46:1-4

It is a good ending to this chapter of the life of Joseph. After being rejected by friends and family, sold as a slave, abused and taken advantage of, thrown into jail only to be freed on order of the king, and rise to the rank of Prime Minister. He then does remarkably well not be bitter and twisted in regard to his brothers, as they arrive to fulfil the dreams he had dreamt as a teenager. The picture is full and the happy ending is in sight as Jacob prepares to finish an earthly journey that has kept him walking through most of the last fifteen chapters of Genesis!

But there is more going on here than at first may be thought. It's good and proper to seek and receive God's guidance on life's plans, but it looks like Jacob had some concerns about moving! And well, rightly so – a whole clan was going on the move, he was old and frail, how would his already proven wayward sons handle the good-life of Egypt, what would be the cost? These things would be on his mind, and also if you go back to chapter 26, Jacob's dad Isaac was not permitted to go to Egypt during the famine when he was alive. God appeared to Isaac and said 'No', now God appears to Jacob and says 'It's OK, go.'

I have a feeling that God still does that – and by that I mean he says different things to different generations. We live in a hugely different world at the end of this century than people lived in during the middle of this century. The last twenty-five years have seen parts of the world move faster than ever before, for example computers. Nowadays it takes a computer one minute to perform a task that twenty years ago took one year. Living in that context, I think it is reasonable to presume God still works in ways and gives us tasks for work in this world. It is our job to find them. It is our job to listen to what God says now, and carry out his will now. God does not always say the same things in the same ways to every generation.

What is God saying today to you and your generation?

Listen carefully . . .

Lord God,
> you are a wondrous Creator,
> wonderful Saviour,
> special friend.
> You protect me
> you guide me,
> you teach me,
> and you give me the will to learn.
> I pray, Jesus, that your Spirit would rule in
> my life,
> that I would be open to what you want to say,
> to me,
> to those around me,
> to the Church,
> to those who hate you,
> to those who don't care about you.
> Lord, here I am,
> I am yours,
> use me
> to live your word,
> today.
> Amen.

GO ON ⟫⟶

1. Are you ever thoughtless regarding the people you live with? (Day 1)

2. What could be done to improve the communication and links between you and those around you?

3. How many ways do you know that people look for a quick profit? (Day 2)

4. Do you think there are ways that people look for spiritual shortcuts – are there such things?

5. Does God use mixed motives for the good of his Kingdom, i.e. is it possible that God is working through us at all times, and not just when we are feeling close to him?

6. It is THE sin . . . And Joseph passes the test. Why does he? (Day 3)

7. If you were in Joseph's position of power, what would you have done?

8. Do you think males and females have different views and thoughts on the area of sexuality? What would the different angles be?

9. Do you ever find it difficult to see how God is using you in your situation? (Day 4)

10. How out of focus do you think the Christian Church is regarding how much thankfulness it gives to God for all it does? How much credit is given to God for the work his people (that's you and me) are trying to do around the globe?

11. How can we make sure people know that God is the source of our meaning and strength?

12. Not a question – but a task. Take some time and write a parable or short story about how things change. (Day 5)

13. Do you know of a church that is doing things especially for your generation? What are they like and does it work? (Day 6)

14. What do you think God is saying to your generation?

15. What are the roadblocks that people face when trying to do the work of God in today's world?

KEEP GOING ⟫→

- God speaking to you in your time – John 1:29-42; Acts 16:6-10

- Family stuff – Psalm 127; Proverbs 22:6; Ephesians 6:14; Luke 2:22-52

- Being greedy – 2 Corinthians 8:7-15; Matthew 19:28-30; Luke 12:13-21

Woman at the well

This is another one of those stories that I remember from way back. It was a regular reading in church and Sunday school, and so of course I knew it well. It has taken on a new meaning lately for me. (Isn't it really good the way the Bible does that . . . God is good, he's so good he keeps us interested!) I shouldn't do this now, but I'm feeling reckless so I'm going to . . . here is the ending right at the beginning.

This encounter I believe is a great microcosm of what happens to a very large number of people when they come 'face to face' with Jesus. It's like a good piece of music, particularly a good jazz piece, it progresses in a definite way. It starts, normal and expected, you can pick out the tune. It goes on and something unexpected happens, the music changes and sounds like it's going somewhere but you cannot pick out exactly where. Then something wonderful happens and the melody is picked up again in a way that we recognise but it's not the same, it's better. It's going somewhere, and we like that. Sometimes, particularly in jazz, the tune can then sound like it gets lost – you may well hear it and think that the melody is gone and can't come back. But then just as things are on the edge it is retrieved in a way that means we almost let out a 'phew, thank goodness'. When a good piece of music is heard in this way, the piece can never be heard the same way again.

This happens to the woman at the well. Things are normal, expected, then she meets Jesus. After a rocky patch, things look like they are going to move forward and just as they do it all seems like it's going to fall apart. For this woman things had to get a lot worse before they could get better. Jesus faced her with who she really was and worked a miracle in her heart. She is only mentioned in John, but she gives us an excellent encounter which many throughout the ages have replicated when meeting the Messiah. And we don't even know her name.

Day 1 ....

The Pharisees heard that Jesus was winning and baptising more disciples than John. (Actually, Jesus himself did not baptise anyone; only his disciples did.) So when Jesus heard what was being said, he left Judaea and went back to Galilee; on his way there he had to go through Samaria. In Samaria he came to a town named Sychar, which was not far from the field that Jacob had given to his son Joseph. Jacob's well was there, and Jesus, tired out by the journey, sat down by the well.

John 4:1-6

Interesting, but really this encounter should never have happened. The well was not in the plan, it was not *en route*. Look over the verses again. The Pharisees had once again been kicking up a fuss, and more than that they had been spreading lies about Jesus. So picture the scene, the disciples say something like, 'You're never going to believe this one Jesus (never a good line to start with when talking to part of the Holy Trinity!), but those boys are saying that you are baptising everyone. *And*, that you and John are in competition. John's behind of course!' The conversation goes on with people chucking in their bit, 'Let's face them with it . . . tell them to get their facts straight . . . they'd better not say anything in front of me or I'll sort them out . . . so what are you going to do Lord? . . . yeah, you've got them this time, they are lying.'

Jesus had them every time.

He leaves, and moves on to let the fuss die down. He does not give a battle cry and march into confrontation. He decides not to harm the work that John is doing for the Kingdom by sticking around. It would have been understandable for Jesus to have been pretty cheesed-off here. He was working in an area, doing good and teaching. And then because of a petty and malicious rumour he moves on. But what happens is not some bitter action plan for the next time he runs into these guys. What happens is that a woman who comes to draw water leaves with a lot more. Even when Jesus is somewhere he didn't plan to be, with every right to be angry. Even when he is somewhere he knew he would not be welcome (Samaritans did not get on with Jews) and even when he is tired from this set of circumstances, he still moves to change the life of some- one who is hurting.

How do we react when situations throw us into places we didn't plan on being?

Jesus,
> your example seems too much at times.
> It's hard enough when you are doing miracles
> and things,
> but when you are being totally human,
> and still doing totally the right thing,
> that makes me feel embarrassed!
> I'm sorry for the times when I've complained,
> I know it's good to do that and tell you about it,
> but maybe it wasn't always necessary.
> Maybe I have been too quick
> to scream about where I find myself sometimes.
> Take these thoughts, Lord,
> and make me into someone
> who can see opportunity
> not road-blocks,
> gates
> not fences,
> doors
> not walls.
> Just like you did.
> Amen.

Day 2

It was about noon. A Samaritan woman came to draw some water, and Jesus said to her, 'Give me a drink of water.' (His disciples had gone into town to buy food.) The woman answered, 'You are a Jew, and I am a Samaritan –

so how can you ask me for a drink?' (Jews will not use the same cups and bowls that Samaritans use.) Jesus answered, 'If only you knew what God gives and who it is that is asking you for a drink, you would ask him, and he would give you life-giving water.'

John 4:7-10

I was doing a bit of shopping in Belfast city centre. It was a Saturday afternoon and it was cold but enjoyable. I bumped into (not literally of course) a very senior minister from the Methodist Church looking at stuff in the window of Habitat – he now lives wondering if I will 'out' him publicly as a Habitat shopper! We were talking about a conference that had just taken place (as you do!) when a married couple who used to go to the church where this minister used to be stationed passed by and stopped. The gentleman quickly took pleasure in the fact that my friend could not remember his name . . . it all began to go wrong from this point.

The gentleman talked and talked, and then began to run Methodists and the Methodist Church into the ground (now I know I've done that, but in working for the Church I think I've earned the right!) This gentleman obviously had barriers in his life. And every time during the conversation his poor wife took a step to the left to make a move away, he started another topic! It eventually got on to the topic of no ministers being able to carry out a service for his local old people's home. My friend gave several suggestions, all positive, as to how a minister may be found for this, all of which were thrown out rather quickly. But the finalé came when the suggestion was aired that the local priest may be asked to do the service. This suggestion was not met with happiness. The words, 'It's a Christian home and we would like it to stay that way,' were heard.

That made me sad.

In the verses above, Jesus breaks through serious religious and cultural barriers. The Samaritans did not speak to the Jews, women did not speak to men, and Samaritan women certainly did not speak to Jewish men. He deals with hundred's of years of misunderstanding, prejudice and superiority. He steps into the arena of division, he does not shy away from religious and cultural barriers, he works to break them down. And when he begins to break them down in this woman's life, she is open to the possibility of what else he could do in her life. We need to deal with our barriers – whatever they may be.

Lord,
I know that there are things inside me
which I am not proud of.
Things that you would help me deal with,
if I asked you.
Things that you want me to change,
things that I'm too scared to let you know about.
That's a bit silly I know – you know everything.
Point out the prejudice in me, Lord.
Show me where I fail in my treatment of those
who go to a different church from me,
those from a different race,
those from a different country,
those who intimidate me for no other reason
than being different from me.
Help me to follow your example in this one.
Amen.

Day 3 ....

'Sir,' the woman said, 'you haven't got a bucket, and the well is deep. Where are you going to get that life-giving water?' . . . Jesus answered, 'Whoever drinks this water will be thirsty again, but whoever drinks the water that I will give him will never be thirsty again. The water that I will give him will become in him a spring which will provide him with life-giving water and give him eternal life.' 'Sir,' the woman said, 'give me that water! Then I will never be thirsty again, nor will I have to come here to draw water.'

John 4:11, 13-15

I've wondered why this woman was so quick to change her mind in this encounter with Jesus. She starts off being cautious, not trusting the strange man beside the well. But within a few verses she is saying, 'Yes, yes, indeed, give me that water so I don't have to come back here again. Tremendous.'

Try this for some thoughts on the matter. Think about why she was at the well at noon – hottest time of the day. Ask why was she alone when gathering water was a job all the women of the village would do together. I think the answer comes in the words of a fourteen year old girl who, when I asked those questions in her class replied, 'She's lonely.'

She is. She has had several husbands, she had probably been messed around and hurt by other men. She was probably the woman who when walking around her village felt the eyes of onlookers in her back. She felt people pointing and talking about her, and she felt rejected. Going to the well by herself was the physical out-working of the pain she was bearing inside. She was alone in many ways. Maybe she thought that if she didn't have to go to the well, perhaps all the pain would stop. So when Jesus told her she would never be thirsty again, she thinks about never having to come to the well. It's what she thinks she needs. If she simply gets her physical/external needs met, then everything in her emotional/internal life would be better.

She's probably not the only one who has ever felt like that. If Jesus came into where you are reading this and offered to do all your homework, all your revision, all the work you have had to bring home, pay all the bills, wouldn't you say, 'Give me that water!' But Jesus wasn't wanting to take care of her physical needs, he wants to go deeper. And he wants to deal deeper with us too. He has business to do on the inside.

Jesus,
I know there are times when you must feel
held to ransom.

'If you get me out of this . . .'
'If mum doesn't find out . . .'
'If they forget about . . . '
I know I've said those prayers, and I'm sorry.
Taking care of what I think I need
is perhaps not the smartest thing to ask for!
Just like this woman at the well thought she knew
what she wanted,
I know that I've not always been on cue
as far as thinking of you and others,
before I've thought of me.
I'd like that to change, Lord.
I'd like to know the right times to ask
and the right things to ask you for.
I think some people call it wisdom.
Help me to grow in it, Lord, under your teaching.
Amen.

Day 4 ....

'Go and call your husband,' Jesus told her, 'and come back.'
'I haven't got a husband,' she answered. Jesus replied, 'You
are right when you say you haven't got a husband. You
have been married to five men, and the man you live with
now is not really your husband. You have told me the truth.'

John 4:16-17

People can say and do the stupidest things at times. I've done several, but alas, writing them now would serve no real purpose ('This has purpose!' I hear you cry!). Around the year 1990 in an American TV magazine, one of the letters on the problem page had the following question: 'Dear Sirs, If we have a nuclear war, will the electromagnetic waves caused by the dropping bombs damage my video tapes?' What! Somehow, I really think that in the event of a nuclear war keeping your video clips may come down the list of priorities. I would hope it would anyway.

Jesus has just faced the woman at the well with what really matters. If you read over yesterday you will recall the type of life she was probably living. Not a pleasant and fulfilling experience. When Jesus tells her to 'Go and get your husband,' that's the weak spot. That's where she hurts the most. That's where Jesus wants to deal with her. Earlier in the encounter things had begun to look better, it was looking good for her. Now things had to get worse for her before they could get ultimately dealt with.

We all put priorities on to different things – hobbies, family, academic qualifications. Jesus wants to be the priority, and he has the right as creator and sustainer to be the priority in our lives. And sometimes when he begins to work with us in our lives, things may get worse for a while before they get better.

Do we open the deepest parts of ourselves to him?

Lord Jesus,
> it's a frightening thought sometimes,
> that you know me better than me.
> I pray that for those emotions and feelings that you
> want to deal with,
> the ones that I try to keep hidden away.
> Here are my thoughts
> and I'm going to try to be honest . . .
> Amen.

Day 5

'I see you are a prophet, sir,' the woman said. 'My Samaritan ancestors worshipped God on this mountain, but you Jews say that Jerusalem is the place where we should worship God.' Jesus said to her, 'Believe me, woman, the time will come when people will not worship the Father either on this mountain or in Jerusalem. . . . But the time is coming and is already here, when by the power of God's Spirit people will worship the Father as he really is, offering him the true worship that he wants. God is Spirit, and only by the power of his Spirit can people worship him as he really is.'

John 4:19-21, 23-24

The reaction of the woman here is reassuringly human. God is offering to deal with her deepest hurts and fears, and she steps into the past to take shelter. The dispute between the Jews and Samaritans had been around since the division of the kingdom of Judah around the year 900 BC – it's now about AD 32. That's a long dispute. And that's where she finds cover. Staying in the past is safe.

There are many other long disputes in this world, many of them going into hundreds of years. I don't have to go very far from home to find a good example of two cultures being suspicious and not trusting each other. When Jesus began to open up the life of this woman at the well, she went to the past to try and hide from present hurts. We still do that today. Jesus says we must humble ourselves and pray and we will receive his blessing, he says we must open ourselves to him and we will experience more than we can ask or think, but we choose to keep ourselves hidden. I know people who, rather than look to a bright new future filled with opportunity, hide in the security of the past. But life moves on . . . it's a basic law of living. John F. Kennedy once said, 'Change is the law of life and those who look only to the past or present are sure to miss the future.'

And it is worth remembering that in the above passage Jesus does not skip the issue for something more important, he still gives the woman an answer to her question of where people should worship. In short his answer is, 'Doesn't matter.'

Lord God,
>   you have so much planned for this world.
>   We must really wreck what you want to do with us.
>   Forgive me for not being clued into what you want,
>   and for hiding in the past.
>   Past failures,
>   past regrets,
>   past stuff I should not have been involved in.
>   And yet it can seem simple there sometimes,

not having to think too much
about changing my ways.
But I know that's not what you want.
I know you have cool stuff planned.
I pray that I can become more clued in
to what you want my future to achieve,
and how I can keep my eyes open,
looking ahead.
I know you will keep working with me on it, Jesus.
Thanks.
Amen.

Day 6 ....

At that moment Jesus' disciples returned, and they were greatly surprised to find him talking with a woman. But none of them said to her, 'What do you want?' or asked him, 'Why are you talking with her?' Then the woman left her water jar, went back to the town, and said to the people there, 'Come and see the man who told me every- thing I have ever done. Could he be the Messiah?' So they left the town and went to Jesus.

John 4:27-30

When I was seventeen I was helping with a Scripture Union summer mission in Scotland. We had a good first week and at the end of it we held an evening service for some of the young people who had been hanging around . . . well, we invited them to our evening service rather than create an evening service for them!

It was informal affair and it was quite meaningful, even up to the point where we split into small groups and spent time praying. During that time a few of the guys who had come along decided that it was time to go. And after they had exited the building, which they were perfectly entitled to do, one of the ladies prayed for these guys. A nice touch you may think. Except that I got the impression from the prayer that the whole leaving scenario had been their doing. And it hadn't. Those in the church had been involved as well. I don't think my friend who was saying the prayer realised that part of the reason they left was because they felt uncomfortable with us.

Jesus has worked a miracle in the life of the woman he met at the well. Then the disciples come back. I like *The Message* translation of verse 28, which states that, 'the woman took the hint and left.' It makes me sad that after all that had happened, the final part of this story (except the woman going back to her village renewed in life) is the disciples getting it so wrong again! You can almost picture their faces . . . suspicious and distrustful of the situation. How sad they were, not yet at the level to be able to click into what their master was doing.

What about churches today? Are we better at it now? Do we accept what Jesus is doing in the lives of all different sorts of people? Or do we give the impression when someone enters our service that they should take the hint and leave? Those guys in Scotland felt they needed to leave – I hope they came back.

Lord Jesus,
    yet again it's another classic mess on our part.
    Times that you work with people,
    changing lives,
    working miracles,
    and we find it hard to see.
    I pray, Lord, that I can be more in tune
    with what you are doing in your world,
    look for where your handiwork is taking place.
    And may I never be unwelcoming
    when anyone comes to your house.
    Because I know deep down, Lord,
    I don't deserve to be there,
    and you let me in.
    Thank you.
    Amen.

GO ON ≫→

1. Have you ever been somewhere where you did not want to be? Ever had to do something you did not want to do? How did you feel? (Day 1)

2. What does it say about the nature of God that in this instance Jesus decides not to stay where he was working – but decides to avoid conflict and move on?

3. Did Jesus always avoid conflict and move on?

4. What dos this setting for the encounter tell us about our everyday Christian journey?

5. What do the actions of Jesus in these verses tell us about how God feels regarding religious and cultural division? (Day 2)

6. Does your faith invite you to tear down misunderstanding and prejudice?

7. What ways can you think of in your situation to begin this process and carry out what Jesus did?

8. Do you feel sorry for this woman? Why? (Day 3)

9. Are there people around where you live/work that you think feel the way this woman did?

10. What are the deepest parts of your life that you keep from Jesus – the ones you think he does not know about? (Day 4)

11. Where and when have you heard people argue that what has gone on in the past is more important than what is going on now? (Day 5)

12. Do you ever step into the past (what has gone on in your life before now) so that you really don't have to face what is happening at the moment?

13. In what ways do you think God is interested in the past?

14. If you had been watching the scene as it unfolded, would you have gone with the disciples in their slightly sceptical line or do you think you would have understood what Jesus was doing? (Day 6)

15. Why do you think the disciples had the reaction they did?

16. Do people nowadays have the same reaction to anything that goes on in Church?

17. What do we learn from this encounter about how God wants us to treat people on the fringes of society? Are we good at it?

KEEP GOING ⋙→

- Division – Galatians 1:6-10; 1 Corinthians 12:12-17
- History – Matthew 5:17-18; 2 Peter 3:1-9
- Judging others – Matthew 7:1-6; Luke 22:24-30

The Rock

There is a rectangular piece of wood on my desk that has the following words engraved into it, 'O Lord, help my words to be gracious and tender today, for tomorrow I may have to eat them.' I cannot bring myself to tell you who bought me that piece of wood or why(!), but I can tell you that at times it has helped me to stop and think before opening my mouth – I know there are some people who will be laughing their heads off after that sentence! I'm glad to be a source of entertainment!

Peter often put his mouth into action before he put his brain into gear. His is an incredible story of transformation from ordinary fisherman to earthly boss of the Christian Church . . . prior to death for refusing to deny his master. It's a story of brilliant success and most dismal failure. It's a story that gives me hope.

There is so much in the New Testament about Peter that it wouldn't be wise to go into scholarly detail (and anyway someone else would have to write it), but here are a few simple instances of his life for you to think about . . .

Day 1 ....

Then Jesus and his disciples went away to the villages near Caesarea Philippi. On the way he asked them, 'Tell me, who do people say I am?' 'Some say that you are Elijah, while others say that you are one of the prophets.' 'What about you?' he asked them. 'Who do you say I am?' Peter answered, 'You are the Messiah.' Then Jesus ordered them, 'Do not tell anyone about me.'

Mark 8:27-30

Basically it's the kind of faith that we all dream of . . . maybe that's unfair of me, I'd better make that personal – it's the kind of faith I dream of. The 'boys' were out on the road having a chat between appearances – the times I'm sure Jesus used in order to have a laugh with his friends as well as teach them. Who knows what they were chatting about? Maybe some people had been shouting abuse in the last town? Maybe some children have run up to one of the 'boys' and said, 'Oy mister, who is he anyway? Can he make me fly?' or maybe some of the women had been giving Jesus the eye (if Jesus was really as popular everywhere he went as the Bible tells us, then you have to admit that many of the women probably would have tried anything to have him as their personal master). We don't know. But we do know that in the conversation Jesus turned and asked them who people thought he was.

Here's a thing – do you think Jesus didn't already know? Why on earth did he have to ask a bunch of people whose greatest tendency was to grab the wrong end of the stick, a serious question like that? Whatever the reason, Peter butts in – I think he was at the back and when he heard the conversation getting serious he couldn't resist jumping into the middle of it – and says words that have been an example to those wishing to be serious followers of Jesus ever since. 'You are the Christ.'

It is worth remembering that for Peter this involved a serious change of historical thought. You see, for him and other Jews, the Messiah was going to be the great deliverer of their hardship. They were under foreign rule (Roman) and they hated it – it had been going on for quite some time by the Babylonians, Persians and Greeks before the Romans. The Messiah was their way out. A great military hero figure who would rid the Jewish people of their oppression. Peter, along with most other Jews, would have been waiting that day with saliva in his mouth!

Jesus, as far as Peter could see, was not raising an army, he was not interested in fighting and power, in fact it seemed that he got authority in doing things in a way totally opposite to the way the Messiah was expected to do them. Peter had to bring his ideas of God into his world. He had to bring his ideas of the Messiah into the face of Jesus, and when he did that his expectations were knocked for six. Peter was able to change his previous ideas in the face of Jesus.

What about our expectations? What do we expect from Jesus? What the minister says every Sunday? What the youth fellowship leader tells you every single week? Let's hope that those things are good and true (for their sake!), but remember that at some time Jesus will look at us and ask, 'Who do you say I am?' No-one else's answer will ever be good enough, the answer has to be ours.

Lord Jesus,
> I love the challenges you give,
> and I love the way you gave them when you were here.
> Thank you that you gave people the opportunity
> to talk to you,
> and you listened,
> and you asked them questions.
> I think it's cool that you shatter expectations,
> and I think I'd like to do that –
> be different for you.
> Help to bring your love to this world,
> in a new exciting way.

I'm sure there are questions you would like to ask me,
and you know I can be a bad listener,
but I'm trying, Lord.
I'm listening . . .
Amen.

Day 2 ....

*Jesus knew that the Father had given him complete power;
he knew that he had come from God and was going to
God. So he rose from the table, took off his outer garment,
and tied a towel round his waist. Then he poured some
water into a basin and began to wash the disciples' feet
and dry them with the towel round his waist. He came to
Simon Peter, who said to him, 'Are you going to wash my
feet, Lord?' Jesus answered him, 'You do not understand
now what I am doing, but you will understand later.' Peter
declared, 'Never at any time will you wash my feet!' 'If I do
not wash your feet,' Jesus answered, 'you will no longer be
my disciple.' Simon Peter answered, 'Lord, do not wash
only my feet then! Wash my hands and head, too!' Jesus
said, 'Anyone who has had a bath is completely clean and
does not have to wash himself, except for his feet.'*

John 13:3-10

Another classic Peter moment. He has come so far and
learnt so much that you would think by now he would
have been getting the picture, but no. You would have
thought that he had watched his Lord heal so many people
that he would not have answered Jesus back. But no. You
would have thought that he may have noticed the change in
Jesus as he drew near to Jerusalem (remember that Jesus
knew what was going to happen there). But no. Having seen
some of the trauma that I think Jesus was going through
here, you would have thought he would just have let Jesus
do what he wanted. But no. You would have thought that
after he had seen Jesus raise people from the dead that he
would not turn round and tell him what he could not do. But

87

no. You would have thought he knew better. But he didn't.

He stands in the face of what Jesus is doing – which if you can picture it is an incredible exercise for the King of Kings, washing dirty feet, euch! By telling Peter that he has no part with him unless he lets him wash his feet Jesus is showing us all the lengths we should go to for each other . . . and it's not easy.

In this narrative we can see that even after three years of living and travelling everywhere with Jesus, Peter could still get it all so wrong. Does that give you hope? It sure helps me.

Then there is just one more question, would you let Jesus wash your feet?

Lord Jesus,
      your example at times can seem so hard.
      Healing and stuff could nearly be easier
      than this humility.
      Thank you for doing it.
      Thank you for helping Peter understand,
      and then me.
      But I do sympathise with Peter a bit,
      because I really wonder whether or not
      I would let you wash mine?
      It sure does cause me to think a bit.
      Above all I want to have a part in you,
      I pray that you would show me just how I can,
      and if it means you have to wash my feet,
      metaphorically of course,
      then I will let you.
      Then I will do the same for others.
      Amen.

Day 3

Then Jesus said to them, 'This very night all of you will run away and leave me, for the scripture says, "God will kill the shepherd, and the sheep of the flock will be scattered." But after I am raised to life, I will go to Galilee ahead of you.'

Peter spoke up and said to Jesus, 'I will never leave you, even though all the rest do!' Jesus said to Peter, 'I tell you that before the cock crows tonight, you will say three times that you do not know me.' Peter answered, 'I will never say that, even if I have to die with you!' And all the other disciples said the same thing.

Matthew 26:31-35

If you didn't know what was going to happen next you would be astounded and inspired by this reading. If you had been there you probably would have shaken your head with the rest of the disciples, I think I would have as well.

Maybe I think too much at times! Because I'm thinking about the power of suggestion, and how if Jesus had said nothing then Peter may have stood a bigger chance of resisting the temptation. Why would Jesus deliberately tell Peter that he was going to fall flat on his face? Why couldn't he just have kept quiet? But then in the end, Jesus wouldn't have been able to forgive him on the beach.

In a way, the ending of this part of Peter's life story ruins it, don't you think? If this dreadful incident in his life had not actually happened, then this small piece of writing would be based on the faith of a saint, a man who when the pressure was really on, stuck to his guns and principles like a bad virus!

Actually, this small piece of writing is about a saint.

Jesus, my Lord,
> I'm glad in a way that you prepared Peter
> for what was to come.
> And I thank you that because you did that
> it enabled him to come back,
> even closer to you.
> I wonder about myself, Lord.
> If I will be able to cut it when it really counts.
> About my ability to really stick in a sticky spot.

I know at the moment I say I hope I could for you,
but Peter said that.
I pray, Lord, that you will give me sensitivity
towards those who have failed you,
towards those who think they couldn't follow you
because they wouldn't make the cut,
and most of all to your Spirit talking to me
and teaching me about myself.
So that I can be better prepared for what is to come.
Amen.

Day 4...

When the disciples who were with Jesus saw what was going to happen, they asked, 'Shall we use our swords, Lord?' And one of them struck the High Priest's slave and cut off his right ear. But Jesus said, 'Enough of this!' He touched the man's ear and healed him.

Luke 22:49-51

Just as well Jesus was there don't you think? Otherwise this poor guy might have bled to death or something! I like to use a bit of licence here from the other Scriptures, because I like to think that it was Peter who drew his sword.

Here's why. While the others are talking and thinking about it, i.e. drawing their swords to protect Jesus, Peter does it – taking matters into his own hands! He is the one who told Jesus only hours ago that he would rather die than leave him, and this is his big chance. Jesus had told Peter he would run away, this was the moment Peter had been waiting for to show Jesus that he had been serious. And so he gets out his sword and cuts off the ear of one of the guards. I also like to think it was Peter because in John's account it says it was!

This account does leave me wondering though. Is there anything that I am doing and getting on with that God thinks I should not be doing? Are there things that Jesus is saying to me not to worry about because they will work themselves out in his time, and yet I get all hot and bothered and in a sense draw a sword?

I actually don't have to think too long about it – I can think of some things God might want me to calm down about straight away. What about you?

Lord God,
  there are so many things that I want to do for you,
  and that I want to get right.
  And maybe I haven't thought to ask what you think.
  I'm sorry for going ahead on my own.
  I know that it must make you sad,
  having great plans for me,
  and yet I manage to keep on motoring
  without listening to you.
  Can I ask, Lord,
  that if I cause some damage to someone,
  the way Peter did,
  that you could fix that too.
  Thanks.
  I pray that you will help me to think a little more,
  before running ahead on my own.
  I'll look more carefully for your signposts.
  Amen.

Day 5 ....

They arrested Jesus and took him away to the house of the High Priest; and Peter followed at a distance. A fire had been lit in the centre of the courtyard, and Peter joined those who were sitting round it. When one of the servant-girls saw him sitting there at the fire, she looked straight at him and said, 'This man too was with Jesus!' But Peter denied it, 'Woman, I don't even know him!' After a little while a man noticed Peter and said, 'You are one of them, too!' But Peter answered, 'Man, I am not!' And about an hour later another man insisted strongly, 'There isn't any doubt that this man was with Jesus, because he is also a Galilean!' But Peter answered, 'Man, I don't know what you are talking about!' At once, while he was still speaking, a cock crowed. The Lord turned round and looked straight at Peter, and Peter remembered that the Lord had said to him, 'Before the cock crows tonight, you will say three times that you do not know me.' Peter went out and wept bitterly.

Luke 22:54-62

If you have never felt like going out and crying then there is no need to read on, you can skip to the next day . . . For those left, which I imagine is actually quite a lot, we are here to recognise we are not alone. It is not a licence, 'OK, Peter screwed up, it's OK for me to do what I want.' No. Peter tried his best but still managed to look into the eyes of Jesus and realise he had let him down hugely. And more significantly, at this point he went and wept bitterly.

What we see from the whole story of Peter, is that Peter was totally human, so are we. Peter messed up big time at certain times and places, but at this time at least, he had the courage to cry – he knew he had done wrong, and he was prepared to start doing something about it. Are we?

I have heard it said by more than one person on more than one occasion, that if you are going to do your best, and if you are going to give your all, then there are going to be times when you hit the floor. It's part of life. A kind of spiritual 'the bigger they are the harder they fall'. Even though he messed up when he got there, at least Peter had made it to the courtyard – the other disciples had run away, and it's not the end yet . . .

I know that I have done stupid things, Lord.
I know I have let you down.
I'm just going to think a while in your presence about some of those times.
Then, I'd like to say sorry . . .
Amen.

Day 6...

After they had eaten, Jesus said to Simon Peter, 'Simon son of John, do you love me more than these others do?' 'Yes, Lord,' he answered, 'you know that I love you.' Jesus said to him, 'Take care of my lambs.' A second time Jesus said to him, 'Simon son of John, do you love me?' 'Yes, Lord,' he answered, 'you know that I love you.' Jesus said to him, 'Take care of my sheep.' A third time Jesus said, 'Simon son of John, do you love me?' Peter was sad because Jesus asked him the third time, 'Do you love me?' so he said to him, 'Lord, you know everything; you know that I love you!' Jesus said to him, 'Take care of my sheep.'

John 21:15-17

Irish singer songwriter extraordinaire Brian Kennedy (each to his own music tastes and all) has sung a song called *Forgiveness* and the question in the chorus is simple, 'Have you ever really known the power of forgiveness?' It's a good song, from a good singer, but there's the question, have you? Peter must have been ecstatic to say the least. He had fallen and fouled up big time and he would have thought that it was all over when Jesus hung on the cross. He would never get to tell him that he was sorry. And so now when the boys are out fishing after the whole episode was drawing to a close (I think it's understandable that they went back to what they knew best, what was familiar) and Jesus appears on the beach, Peter jumps into the water and gets to shore as fast as he can.

It must have been some breakfast on the beach. Peter's mind must have been working overtime because this was the first time he has seen Jesus since he looked in to his eyes at the moment of failure, and he must have thinking 'Hmm, what is he going to say?'

How many of us feel the same? We worry about all that Jesus knows about us! The fact that God is above and beyond time and space is a terrifying thing rather than a freeing one. We are intimidated by God knowing everything about us – at least I am. But then I read how Jesus treated Peter here. I picture them going for a walk and a chat along the beach. The marvellous thing is that Jesus does not make Peter squirm and feel horrible (Jesus knows he has done enough of that) he simply asks him does he love him. Three times for three denials. Peter can look into his eyes and say yes. Jesus made the move, Jesus stretched his hands and Peter accepted his love. Peter experienced forgiveness.

Of course it does not end here. Peter goes on to be one of the most important men in the earthly church. He still made mistakes (read all about the Jews/Gentiles debate in Acts) and God still had changes to make in his life. But he went on as a warrior for Christ and died for his Lord.

Lord Jesus,
    you give so much to us.
    You gave your life,
    and you continually give us your hand to hold,
    your ear to turn to,
    and your Spirit to help us.
    Thanks for showing me that there is always
    an easy channel to you.
    I hope I can use it more often!
    I pray, Lord, that you would receive my prayer
    for forgiveness,
    as I tell you
    I love you.
    Amen.

GO ON ≫→

1. What expectations do people you know have of Jesus? Do they have the same expectations for the Church? (Day 1)

2. How have your expectations of Jesus changed since you got to know him better?

3. If you had been in the room during this last supper, and you had watched Jesus wash the disciples' feet, what would you have thought? Would you have wanted to tell Jesus anything? What would you have said to Peter after he told Jesus 'no'? (Day 2)

4. This is a real lesson on service for the disciples. Look around at yourself, your church, your minister/leaders – how are we getting on in the light of this lesson?

5. How many ways can you think of to 'wash people's feet?' And if you can think of some, what is stopping you?

6. Can you relate to that sense of mountain-top security that Peter seems to have? Where did you get the strength? Where do you think Peter got the strength? (Day 3)

7. Do you know people who have the same kind of strength of faith as Peter in this passage? Where are they, what are they doing?

8. Take a look around you . . . Think about your life and the things you do for God. Do you do a lot of things in church? Do you do anything in church or for a voluntary organisation? How cluttered is your life with the things you do for God? (Day 4)

9. Are there things that you can think of that God wants some people to stop doing – things that the people doing them think are good and holy?

10. What does Jesus' reaction to Peter in the passage tell you about anger? Was Jesus ever angry?

11. Can you relate to letting anyone down that you cared about? How did it feel? (Day 5)

12. What do the tears that Peter shed here tell us about him, and his experiences of Jesus?

13. How do you think Jesus felt about Peter at this time? How does he feel about us when we screw up?

14. Do you think Peter was nervous about talking to Jesus again? (Day 6)

15. Do people living nowadays understand this type of love that comes from Jesus?

16. What is the offshoot of the forgiveness that comes from Jesus?

17. Have you ever experienced this forgiveness? If not, why not?

KEEP GOING ≫→

- Forgiveness – Luke 6:37; Ephesians 4:30-32; Matthew 18:21-35

- Strength from above – Ephesians 3:14-19; James 3:13-18; Ephesians 2:15-23

- Failure – Moses: Exodus 2:11-16 Noah: Genesis 9:20-21 Cross check with Hebrews 11:7, 27-28

Rich young ruler

Four years ago I was involved in running an Easter event for young people in my home town of Bangor, Co. Down – whaaey! (Bangor boys do that . . . apparently!). It was an event that was really special and it has continued over the years with a real sense of God being present – a totally cool youth thing. Anyway, near the end of that first week, we were getting the band ready and starting things up for the evening praise event when we had a young man come in, with his dog. He had been on something, and was doped up to the eyeballs. He walked around and seemed to want to play every instrument as the band started. He stumbled around in front of the hundred or so teenagers and created a fuss. No one really knew quite what to do. And I was meant to be in charge of this whole thing.

I don't know how well we handled the disruption – I don't know if there is ever a good way to deal with that kind of disruption. But a couple of the guys on the door managed to persuade him to hang about with them for a while instead of playing with the band! Later, the police arrived and he sat on the doorsteps of the church with them for a time, before stumbling somewhere else.

A couple of weeks later I was talking about the incident with my mum, who had been there. She and dad had been driving home and had seen him with his dog walking down the deserted main street. It was pouring with rain. She told me it looked a sad sight. I felt sad as she told me.

Soon afterwards I was reminded that Jesus had let people walk away. I don't know if it makes me feel better about that night in Bangor, but I know that it happened. I can read about it in three out of the four Gospels, and since that night I have read over it many times, asking why? I'm not sure I have a good answer, but I do have some thoughts. And in a world where many people do walk away from Jesus, it is something I need to think about – because as a Christian I have to stop people walking away.

Day 1 ....

As Jesus was starting on his way again, a man ran up, knelt before him, and asked him, 'Good Teacher, what must I do to receive eternal life?' 'Why do you call me good?' Jesus asked him. 'No one is good except God alone.'

Mark 10:17-18

I know a minister who is crazy about sport – I'd like to be but I'm just not built that way! Several years ago there was a huge rugby match on in Dublin, and it was for Ireland to win the Triple Crown. All day the minister was out whilst he recorded the match on video, and all day he asked people not to tell him the result. He went to great lengths to not hear the score . . . he even crossed the street to avoid looking into shops that had TVs in the window. When he got home in the evening he put on the video and began to watch one of the most nail-biting matches Ireland has been involved in for years. It got so tense in the second half that he just couldn't handle it, so he fast-forwarded to find out the score! It all just got too tense.

As I read the verses above, I think the rich young ruler has that same sense of urgency and tension. He runs to Jesus, as Jesus is getting ready to go, and he falls on his knees before him – if that does not portray a sense of urgency I don't know what does. But what Jesus says next does make me wonder. The ruler calls him 'good teacher'; Jesus asks him why he calls him this, then, more than that, says that it is only God who is good. But we know Jesus is God, so why is he saying it?

Part of the answer is in the writer. In the whole of his Gospel Mark does not have any human being address Jesus as the Son of God before the crucifixion. I think it is a great writing device to help bring out the real truth of the good news – only after everything has happened to the promised Messiah that the prophets foretold is the truth revealed to humanity. Kind of like the end of a play where only in the end is the hero vindicated and the wicked king is seen for all he is and finally defeated. It is interesting that at the end of this Gospel it is the soldier at the foot of the cross who realises what had actually happened.

Another part of the answer to the question above is in the heavenly signpost! Here was a young man, who had been successful in all he had done. He was rich, he was probably known and popular around his area and maybe was even feared a bit. But something inside was missing, all was not well with the soul. That's why he came to Jesus. And that's why when he addresses Jesus as less than he is, Jesus points to where the ultimate answers really are. Not in any earthly teacher, but in the Almighty Father.

Where do we send people with the big questions of life?

Lord Jesus,
    there are parts of your Bible
    that I have to think about a bit.
    And the start of this encounter is one of those parts.
    But I like the way you handled people,
    easily and helpfully.
    Wanting to give them even more
    than they were asking,
    helping them realise what they were really wanting.
    I know there are times when I ask 'what's it all about?'
    Times when I feel like I just want to fall at your feet
    and question you.
    Thank you that when I do that,
    you listen to what I say.
    And thank you for pointing this ruler
    to where the answers lie,
    to where in the end, life does make sense.
    So many people look for meaning in so many places,
    and sometimes I look for meaning
    outside of you, Lord.
    I'm sorry for the times I have thought
    I could create meaning myself.

You are the Lord,
you reign on high.
Let it be,
for ever.
Amen.

Day 2 ....

'You know the commandments: Do not commit murder; do not commit adultery; do not steal; do not accuse anyone falsely; do not cheat; respect your father and your mother.' 'Teacher,' the young man said, 'ever since I was young, I have obeyed all these commandments.' Jesus looked straight at him with love . . .

Mark 10:19-21

If there was any doubt about this young man's sincerity, this should put it to rest. Not only did he grab Jesus as he was moving on to somewhere else, and not only did he fall at the feet of Jesus, but now we know that he meant business with this spiritual life – he had even kept all the commandments since he was a young man. And not too many of us can say that!

But here's the problem – he hadn't kept the commandments. We know that because we know the Bible tells us we have all sinned against God. This young man with all the good intentions in the universe could not have kept the whole law. It is at this point that I can picture the disciples in the background sniggering.

You see, in the previous couple of chapters they had been seriously told off a couple of times by Jesus. They had watched Jesus healing, teaching, talking to Moses and Elijah, and they had still managed to argue amongst themselves as to who was the greatest, they had also tried to stop children coming to Jesus. To use good Ulster language, Jesus had 'laid into them'! The disciples could well have thought that this young man was about to get the same kind of earful. 'Oh yeah – you think you've done it all, kept up to date – well you haven't laddie, you are no nearer the Kingdom because of all that effort. You are blinded to the meaning of life and you will never see the meaning of true peace through the meaningless following of tedious ritual and mindless observation of tired tradition.' Or something like that.

They would have been disappointed. Jesus looked at the young man and he loved him. He looked at his striving, he looked at his searching, he looked at his efforts, which although he was young were already becoming tired, and he looked at his heart. That's where he deals with the young man's problem (but that's another day!). Jesus looked, listened and loved. Do you treat people you meet like that? I've never been brilliant at it – but I'm still trying.

> There are times, Lord, when I feel tired of trying.
> There seems to be so much to get right.
> So much that I need to do.
> So many ways to trip up.
> So many ways to fail.
> There is no way I could even think of saying
> what this young man said,
> I'm nowhere near keeping your law.
> But I'm trying.
> I want to treat people the way you treated them.
> Listening, looking to the real person
> and not outer appearance.
> Loving people simply because they come from you.
> Help me in my trying, Jesus.
> Amen.

Day 3 ....

Jesus looked straight at him with love and said, 'You need only one thing. Go and sell all you have and give the money to the poor, and you will have riches in heaven; then come and follow me.' When the man heard this, gloom spread over his face, and he went away sad, because he was very rich.

Jesus looked round at the disciples and said to them, 'How hard it will be for rich people to enter the Kingdom of God!'
Mark 10:21-23

This is the only recorded time in the Gospels that anyone did walk away from Jesus. I'm sure there were more. And I know that every day in this world people walk away from Jesus. They decide that it's not worth it. I'm sure they think they have their reasons. The only recorded reason in the Gospel is this one – he left because Jesus asked too much of him. He was rich, he was successful, and he was young. He felt that it wasn't worth it.

Isn't it interesting that the only recorded reason for not following Jesus when he asks is too much money. What I find interesting in other parts of the Bible is that money and pleasure are seen as blessings from God. Go look at Job 1:10; or Psalm 128:1-2. In other times and other places, the love and misuse of money brings about a curse from God – Amos 5:10-13. So what is it about this young man that makes it all so bad? It probably is the problem that money has become this young man's priority, it's what he is, money defines him. We don't even know his name, he is the 'rich young man'. Money is his lot. And Jesus asks him to lose it for the sake of the Kingdom.

Remember Jesus looked at the heart – this is what he saw. This is what was wrong – his priorities were screwed up, everything was the wrong way round. And the young man could not bring himself to turn them the right way round. The thing is, it's such an easy thing to get caught into – living life the wrong way round.

God tells us that he has given us life, life in all its fullness. And what do we see as we look around at the lives God has given us? People who care more about getting rich quickly than they do about millions of children who die every year from starvation; people who care more for geographical borders than they care about human life; people who care more about living life hard tonight by popping a tab, rather than the knowledge that drugs can kill – they may never get tomorrow.

It's the disease of LSS – Life Short Sightedness.

What are your priorities?

It makes me sad, Lord, that people walk away from you.
I don't really understand how they could prefer
having loads of cash
to knowing peace and fulfilment with you.
But then I'm young and I don't have a lot of it!
I wonder what I would do if you wanted me
to give some away
and it scares me a bit.
It's the kind of question I'm not easy thinking about,
and I know that's wrong.
I know that I get things turned around in my head,
and things that really don't matter seem huge.
Sorry, Lord.
You are my priority, and I love you.
Over the coming days and months,
show me how I can serve you better,
and draw closer.
Give me ears to hear.
Amen.

Day 4 ....

The disciples were shocked at these words, but Jesus went on to say, 'My children, how hard it is to enter the Kingdom of God! It is much harder for a rich person to enter the Kingdom of God than for a camel to go through the eye of a needle.'

Mark 10: 24-25

The image the media would have us believe is that it cures all our problems, leaves us with the chance to get anything we want when we want it, it can cure our ills. And as I dream and think about it I do bad things! I think that it would be nice to be able to come home and if I've had a bad day, lie in the Jacuzzi, or sit in the sauna – get a drink from the bar beside the pool in the downstairs leisure suite, and listen to some MTV on the multi-TV wall. See what I mean, I do bad things when I start that. I don't think I'm alone either, I think there are many people who dream about money in a much bigger and a lot more serious and sinister way than I do. I don't dream about having lots of it, that's only a gag. But I do worry occasionally about that sinking stomach feeling that comes from not having it. And I've never experienced real poverty – I can't imagine what it would be like – and I think it would be patronising to try. But for all those dreamers, think on these words: millionaire Andrew Carnegie said, 'Millionaires seldom smile.' And did you know that the first person to win the national lottery in Britain said they wished they could give it all back?

Money is not evil – 'the love of money is the root of evil.' It's OK to have money, it's OK to spend money. But there are some things we should remember every day. Considering we can't take it with us when we go, considering that those of us who have money are in the minority of the world, considering that the only person to walk away from Jesus in the Gospel did so because he had lots of money, don't you think we need to take the whole idea a lot more seriously than we do? Jesus leaves us in no doubt as to what he thinks about storing up money – and it's fairly serious.

Heavenly Lord,
    this is another thing that makes me feel guilty!
    I bought a new pair of combats last week,
    and I probably paid too much.
    There are a load of things that I think I need,
    and I probably really don't . . .
    In fact there is no way I need half of them.
    It's a big area of my life, Lord,
    and I need you to help me get it right,

there is hardly anything
that doesn't cost money nowadays,
entertainment, fun, food, water!
Give me wisdom as to how I spend,
and what I save,
but more importantly,
what I give to you, and how I give it.
I know there are places and people
that need my help,
help me to find them.
I'm starting to look now, Father . . .
Amen.

Day 5...

At this the disciples were completely amazed and asked one another, 'Who, then, can be saved?' Jesus looked straight at them and answered, 'This is impossible for man, but not for God; everything is possible for God.' Then Peter spoke up, 'Look, we have left everything and followed you.'

'Yes,' Jesus said to them, 'and I tell you that anyone who leaves home or brothers or sisters or mother or father or children or fields for me and for the gospel, will receive much more in this present age. He will receive a hundred times more houses, brothers, sisters, mothers, children and fields – and persecutions as well; and in the age to come he will receive eternal life.'

Mark 10:26-30

I think Peter had that certain feeling that something was not going right! A few weeks back I was at one of my sisters' house. The previous day I had been on a youth weekend and so I was a bit wrecked . . . aaahhhhh. Yeah, yeah. Anyway, I went up to my five-year-old nephew's bed and had a lie down. (Yes, I know only old people do that – but this was an exception!) After a while of relative peace I felt something crawling up my leg . . . not a little thing, but quite a big thing. I woke up and found the cat looking at me with a 'listen – neither of us is meant to be here so if you don't say anything then I won't either' look on his face. So I cuddled down again. It was then I saw Michael, my nephew, standing at the door wondering what to do . . . this was all wrong, Uncle Jools was in bed and he should be downstairs running about and being an adult! After a minute or so of eyeing up the situation (he didn't know I was only half asleep and could see him) he did the only thing a five-year-old could do in that situation. He screamed, ran towards the bed and jumped on his uncle. Understandable.

So is this outburst of Peter's. He has listened and watched the whole episode unfold. He has watched an encounter where he hadn't a clue what was going to happen, and he had seen Jesus let a young man walk away. He has listened as Jesus said that people cannot get into the Kingdom themselves, and I think he and the other disciples had taken enough for one day, so he pipes up and finally asks, 'What about us?' He wouldn't be the only one throughout history either. Countless people, including me if I'm being honest, have cried out, 'What about me – am I going to be all right?' So what about us – are we going to be all right?

The answer is in the words around the question – if we are left to ourselves no, but we are not left to ourselves, God is with us. For encouragement, Jesus goes on to add that people who lose things in this life will not only gain in the Kingdom, they will gain now. Isn't it great to remember that God will not wait until we're in heaven to look after us.

Jesus,
>I've felt strange at times about you.
>I've wondered about giving my all to you,
>and I've wondered about what it would mean
>to be looked after by you.
>I suppose when I think about it,
>you've never let me down.

Thank you.
And thank you
that you never will.
I pray that you will help me trust
in what you will provide,
because I know
you care for me,
and I know your will is the way of life.
Help me to be always thankful
and always remembering what you have given.
Keep my eyes open
to see what you have done.
Keep my ears open
to listen about what you have done.
And keep my lips ready to tell about
what you have done.
Thanks, Lord.
Amen.

Day 6 ....

But many who now are first will be last, and many who now are last will be first.

Mark 10:31

One of the biggest questions that goes with us through life is the question of our dreams. It's a really bad measure of our society that a lot of people do not feel they can dream – a dose too much cynicism, a heavy spoonful of doubt, a serious helping of reality . . . whatever the reason we have lost our ability to 'dream our dreams.'

I think dreams help us to know there can be a better tomorrow. In one sense the Kingdom of God is our dream as a Christian. It's what we wish to happen fully and completely here on earth, it's a fantastic look at what can be instead of what is. The verse above is a signpost to one of the major values of that Kingdom. The last are going to be first, and vice versa. But what does that mean to me today?

There was a guy I went to school with for about eight years or so. He went to my primary school and then we went to the same grammar school. We were never buddy-buddies, but we knew each other, liked each other (I think!) and then he left our school after GCSEs to go to another 'bigger' school. Whenever we saw each other after that we always had a laugh and at times quite deep and meaningful chats. But life for him was due to be all too short.

Something somebody told me about him a week after he had been tragically killed falling off a high cliff in Donegal, I always want to remember. He had been on a church weekend and they were discussing dreams and hopes for the future. The leader had asked them to write down what they wanted to achieve over the next ten, fifteen and twenty years. The leader wanted their answers. My friend wrote: 1. Know Jesus better. 2. Know Jesus better. 3. Know Jesus better.

That is the kind of dreaming that has inspired me. It's also about the last coming first, and the first trying to get themselves to the back – it's knowing Jesus, it's dreaming his dreams for this world.

Lord,
    you know I find bits of your Bible hard.
    You know there are things in it that I probably ignore,
    because I think I couldn't do them.
    This was one of those verses, Lord.
    There are so many people clamouring about,
    going fast,
    just to be first.
    I pray that you will give me a vision of your Kingdom,
    where things are turned upside down,
    and back to front.
    I want to know you better, Jesus.
    I want to love you more,
    I want to dream your dreams for this place.
    Help me do that, Lord,
    give me the dreams.
    Amen.

GO ON ⋙→

1. What do you think the big questions of life are? (Day 1)

2. Have you managed to answer them all?

3. Where are you looking for answers? Where do you send people who are looking for answers?

4. What kind of things do other people do that convince you they are wrong? (Day 2)

5. After reading the above passage, how do you think Jesus feels about them – and more importantly, how do you think Jesus wants us to feel about them?

6. It is so often said that as people get older they forget the dreams and ideals of their youth. But the above story plainly states that the problem of money was with a young man – how can we, as young people, show older generations that we are serious about what Jesus says in this passage? (Day 3)

7. Are you prepared to believe that because the Bible says Jesus told someone to 'sell all he had and give the money to the poor', Jesus might say the same to people today?

8. What stops people giving all that they have and are in a post-modern world?

9. Think of the dreams you have for moving forward in life – what are they, where do they take you? (Day 4)

10. Do they involve having lots of money to do them? Why/why not?

11. Are there times when you feel that God isn't listening and does not care? (Day 5)

12. How do you feel about God in times like that? How do you feel about yourself in times like that?

13. We do not enter the Kingdom of God for reward points – how does it make you feel that Jesus reassures the disciples that they will have more in this life than they

could imagine? And yet some of them were martyred for their faith – what do you think Jesus is talking about?

14. It's a strange statement to make, but what does the statement 'dreaming to be last' say to you? (Day 6)

15. How can we strive daily to 'know Jesus better' in light of the story of the rich young ruler?

16. In terms of your Church life, who are the first and who are the last – is it the right way round? Where do you put yourself?

17. In terms of the society where we live, who are first and who are the last – is it as it should be? How can we do something about it if it's not?

KEEP GOING ≫→

• Dreaming dreams – Joel 2:28-29; Joshua 1:9

• Money – Acts 8:14-23; John 2:13-17; Haggai 1:4-6

• Priority – Ecclesiastes 11:9-10; Genesis 22:1-18

Paul

I know that I have probably offended some people by trying to get some major figures of the Bible into just six meditations – aw well, sorry. I don't claim to have given any special 'shortcut learning' to Bible success. But if it is always difficult to fit Bible characters into limited space – it really is totally impossible to fit the story of the apostle Paul into six meditations. So I'm not going to try. This chapter is just a little different.

Paul was probably the greatest evangelist and missionary that ever lived. He travelled all around his known world in an effervescent effort to tell people about the Gospel of Christ. He wasn't liked by everyone. He was put in jail several times, beaten, run out of towns, caused riots, was shipwrecked, and in his own inimitable style he left behind more than one travelling companion. All of this was done in between writing what ended up as most of the New Testament. He was a remarkable individual.

He also has other attributes that bring him to people's attention. He did not appear to have a lot of time for women in the early church (reminding Timothy in his first letter that it was Eve who ate the apple), and the regulations that Paul places on lifestyle would give even the keenest observers of Christianity a difficult time today. Writers and scholars have enjoyed debating his writings for years, and they will probably continue to do so.

The following meditations are picked out from several different letters he wrote. They are not meant to give a cross-divisional view of Paul, and they are not designed to give an overview of his theology, but are simply written to give spiritual food to chew on, and I hope they are encouraging for you – just remember what he was doing before he started writing!

Day 1 ....

Do not let anyone look down on you because you are young, but be an example for the believers in your speech, your conduct, your love, faith, and purity. . . . Practise these things and devote yourself to them, in order that your progress may be seen by all.

1 Timothy 4:12, 15

It was the first service I had been asked to take part in as an employee of the Methodist Church; it was a bit frightening, it was in a small rural congregation, it was also the last service of worship I wore a suit to – it just wasn't me.

I was sitting in the public gallery of the Methodist conference listening to the youth report. I had just witnessed a couple of hundred ministers walk into the conference floor on one of the hottest days of the year so far, and they were all wearing grey or dark blue suits. As I watched from the gallery, one minister walked onto the conference floor in his denims – jacket and jeans! The President leaned over to the acting secretary and asked 'Should he be in here?'

A Presbyterian minister was asked to go and speak in a special service. He wore a jacket and tie, although he hates them. At the end of the sermon, on reaching out and embracing young people around them, he informed the congregation of his tie struggle and told them that he wore it so that they would listen to him. How true, and sad.

I don't think that when Paul encourages us to be examples to those in the church he was talking about what we wear. He was going a lot deeper than that. It's about attitude and lifestyle. It's about how we forgive, how we have a reverence in church that doesn't lose the command of God to 'party' at times; it's about getting the most of the life that God has given, offering all that we have and are to him and his Kingdom. If young people all around Britain and Ireland stand up for Jesus in their churches and live lives that shine Christ, there will be one serious move of God in these lands. Go on, dare you . . . be an example.

Lord God,
   thank you for being amazing.
   A loving and caring friend,
   someone who hears all my thoughts,
   sees all my actions,
   feels my hurt,
   knows my pain.
   And does not run away.
   I really long to watch your Spirit move in these lands,
   and the thought of being an example is really exciting.
   I pray that I will know you are with me
   if people slam me for being young.
   And I pray that I can have understanding and wisdom
   in dealing with older sisters and brothers in you.
   Lord, may we all see your grace at work.
   Amen.

Day 2 ....

If he has done you any wrong or owes you anything, charge it to my account. Here, I will write this with my own hand: I, Paul, will pay you back.

Philemon 18, 19

The whole book of Philemon is a plea from Paul on behalf of a friend. Onesimus had been a slave to Philemon, somehow he had escaped and run away from his master, and when he met Paul on his journey, he had become a Christian. The whole piece of writing is an appeal to Philemon to take Onesimus back as a forgiven slave and also as a brother in Christ. So what, if anything, does this have to say to me today?

I feel sure that a few hundred years ago this book had a lot to say to a society where slavery was an accepted norm.

I'm glad it's not like that in Ireland today. Sadly, I would feel sure there were Christians who, when the calls came (from only a few to begin with) to get rid of slavery in this country, they pointed to this book and said, 'Paul said it's OK to have slaves – it's in the Bible – have you read Philemon?' I'm not sure how I would have responded. But I really don't think that what Paul is doing in this letter is arguing the case for slavery – the point of the letter is in the verse above.

Paul is showing that Onesimus has met with the living Lord, and as such is amongst the fellowship of believers. He is one of them. Paul reminds Philemon (strongly in places) what his own debt to Paul is – presumably Paul had something to do with the conversion of Philemon, and in doing so writes off the whole debt issue in favour of an issue of love.

The bold preacher, teacher, traveller, and outstanding Christian is taking someone else's debt on his shoulders – literally. He has been responsible for the conversion of hundred's of people, he has established a large number of churches, and he stood up in Acts 15 and told Peter he was wrong! And yet here he is showing something even more important than all of that, something that really counts. Are we that willing to put our faith where our mouths are?

Lord Jesus,
    I know you've got special things for us all to do.
    And I know
    that all we do is special.
    I pray, Lord,
    that I can learn about all the things I can do.
    Not just the big things that people see,
    the things they remember,
    like collecting for charity,
    doing drama in church,
    playing in the band,
    leading a small group
    and going to the prayer meeting,

but the things where I can really help in a real way, like Paul did for Onesimus.
Thanks for showing me that.
Amen.

Day 3 ....

I do not claim that I have already succeeded or have already become perfect. I keep striving to win the prize for which Christ Jesus has already won me to himself. Of course, my brothers, I really do not think that I have already won it; the one thing I do, however, is to forget what is behind me and do my best to reach what is ahead.

Philippians 3:12-13

I think people are way too concerned with winning these days! Just look at the expectation on the English football team over the last few years – since they failed to get to the World Cup in '94 (tee-hee-hee). Things are not just a game anymore, if you can play snooker, tennis, darts, or just about any other sport really well you could make an absolute packet out of it. Loadsamoney!

Paul reminds us to keep humble about the whole life thing. None of us are perfect, none of us are at a stage where God has finished working with us, none of us have 'made it'. And to be totally honest I am always fairly aware and sceptical of those who give the impression they think they have 'made it.' I am nowhere near perfect – and I imagine you are fairly far away yourself. (But I don't like to be too presumptuous.)

It's good for me to hear Paul talking about not being there yet, and it is also good for me that Paul tells me those things in the past that keep dragging me down do not have to be chains. We cannot escape what we have gone through – we need to learn as we travel. But that does not mean we let the mistakes and regrets of the past ruin our today. That happens with a lot of Christian people. It's gone, it's done, and it's dealt with. I have done things in the past I'm not proud of, and I know you probably have to, but we have to let go of them and not look back. In that way we will be able to face what happens next without the extra load of what we are still carrying.

Daddy God
> you know just about everything I've done,
> and I do.
> You know everything better than me.
> You have told me in the Bible
> that you have dealt with sin
> if we give it to you.
> I know there are things I hang on to.
> And that's not good, is it, Lord?
> I want to keep travelling,
> and get to the end.
> I want to do as well as I can for your Kingdom,
> but at times things from behind can get too heavy.
> Help me, Lord,
> to be like you,
> to leave things when they are dealt with.
> To look forward,
> and to stop getting a sore neck
> from always looking backwards.
> In your precious name I pray.
> Amen.

Day 4...

I am surprised at you! In no time at all you are deserting the one who called you by the grace of Christ and are accepting another gospel. Actually, there is no 'other Gospel,' but I say this because there are some people who are upsetting you and trying to change the gospel of Christ. But even if we or an angel from heaven should preach to you a gospel that is different from the one we preached to you, may he be condemned to hell!

Galatians 1:6-8

So, what are you trying to say, Paul? This is fairly strong language, and in the Greek it's not really a pleasant passage – it comes across a lot stronger than it does even in English. So what is he upset about?

The people of Galatia seemingly had a special part in Paul's heart, he only stayed in one place longer than he stayed in Galatia, and I think he felt a real burden for them – a responsibility.

He learns while he is ministering somewhere else that some believers are moving away from the original and best . . . a bunch of people named the 'Judaisers' are the problem. They were a group who followed Paul and preached a gospel that was decidedly 'Jewish' in its outlook. That is to say, the gospel of grace and love was out the window and a gospel of hard work and effort to try and get to heaven was back. Paul reacts against this very strongly. He later goes on to remind the Galatians that it is only by faith that we are put right with God. The people of Galatia needed to hear it, and so do we today.

We get very caught up in the right and wrongs of daily Christian living – and yes, it is important that we try and live the life we believe to be pleasing to God. But that's not what gets us to the big party in the sky. That's not what changes the world, and it is certainly not why I feel I can write meditations about us and God. It's because I have received grace. It's because no matter how hard I try I can never make it to the God standard. It's because no matter how high I jump I'm always short of heaven. We all are. The great thing is, while it's depressing to think of how bad we are, God has provided the means to bring us to him, and to bring his Kingdom fully on earth. And it's free. It cost God everything, but he gives it to us for free.

No wonder Paul was upset about those who wanted to add to that message.

Jesus,

thank you.

Your life and love are incredible to me.

And I know it's all I need.
Lord, in the quietness I want to once again
place myself before you,
and give you my all.
Here I am . . .
All for you, Jesus.
Amen.

Day 5

I may be able to speak the languages of men and even of angles, but if I have no love, my speech is no more than a noisy gong or a clanging bell. I may have the gift of inspired preaching; I may have all knowledge and understand all secrets; I may have all the faith needed to move mountains – but if I have no love, I am nothing.

1 Corinthians 13:1-2

There is a story told about a famous evangelist who was travelling in America. As part of his tour he was preaching at special open air evangelistic meetings in a large town. Every evening he did his sermon and people responded, and people were saved because of his work.

On one of the last days of the mission, the evangelist decided to take a run around town by himself for a while. He went to different places and saw different things about the life of this large town – and he saw some of their problems.

As the time came for the evening event, the evangelist was not back. The organisers were getting anxious, and they sent people out looking for him. He was nowhere to be found. All the stewards and those involved in the organisation were soon out on the streets looking for this man, yet he still could not be found. Eventually, one of the organisers came across the evangelist in a small dirty flat in the 'bad' part of town. He was sitting with a woman and her baby, who were in obvious distress, and he was ministering to her. The man who had found him spoke in quite harsh terms, 'The meeting has already started and we need you there . . . can you please come now, we have people to do this.' And the evangelist replied, 'Yes, you do, but they were not doing it.'

It's really easy to get into traps, but we can never lose what the Gospel of Jesus says about human beings, and about love. What Paul says is simple, 'I could be able to do everything in the whole wide world, have it all, and get it right, but without love – totally nothing.'

Jesus,
> I know that there is a lack of that in me!
> I know I'm not loving enough,
> I know I hurt people,
> I offend you, and I do myself damage.
> But this is me, Jesus,
> and I know I can't change.
> Not without your help.
> So here's the difficult prayer,
> help me to be more loving, Lord,
> because I know that's what makes the difference.
> Amen.

Day 6 ....

In view of all this, what can we say? If God is for us, who can be against us?

Romans 8:31

I think that's the question – that's it, that's the one. It's the one we all want to know, it's the one we find hardest to believe, it's the one that can give us the most comfort. It's the one I find myself going to time and time again.

Think for a minute . . . if you were Paul, and you wanted to express the greatness and grace of God how would you have done it?

You want your readers to know that there is nothing higher, greater, deeper, better than the Lord. You want people to know that in his hands there is not just rest and peace for those who find it difficult today, but there is safety and care for those who struggle everyday, and better than that, there is a hope that is for tomorrow, what's more it will never fade, it will never go away, it will never stop. It is eternal.

You want to communicate to those who will hear it that Jesus, the son of the almighty God became human. He left the comfort, safety, glory, pleasure, and splendour of the heavens to be like us. He got up from a throne of eternity and sat in a feeding trough. He decided not to listen to the unending hymns of praise, and opted to hear people shout for his death. He went from being clothed in all that is good and holy, to being clothed in a red robe. He left a crown of dazzling brilliance to have a crown of thorns placed on his head.

You need people to know that this was done for them and that there is nothing, absolutely nothing that can ever stop the powerful creating God of the universe from loving them. He is always going to be on their side, he will come when they call. What would you have written?

I think Paul does all right, don't you?

Thank you, Lord.
Let it be,
now and for ever.
Amen

Day 7 ....

So then, my brothers, because of God's great mercy to us I appeal to you: Offer yourselves as a living sacrifice to God, dedicated to his service and pleasing to him. This is the true worship that you should offer.

Romans 12:1

I would have to confess that when I was younger, the term 'living sacrifice' really did cause me some bother. I remember hearing it said and sung about in Sunday school, and all I could think of was the poor little lambs that the old people in the Old Testament used to stick on the altar! I wasn't exactly sure what being a living sacrifice entailed, but you could be flippin' sure that for me there was going to be no sitting on an altar waiting to be chopped or burned.

Of course, years later it all makes sense. It's simple really. (Yeah, right!) In the Old Testament, sacrifice was used to enable the people to draw closer to God. It was a form of worship whereby they gave something special that they had grown or raised, and as a sign of their commitment to God they would give it back to God as an offering. There was one particular sacrifice where the sins of the people were placed on a goat and the goat was put to wandering in the desert. You can also read in the Old Testament about how a lot of these sacrifices were not pleasing to God, because on the one hand the people were sacrificing animals, while on the other they were cheating the poor or taking advantage of those less fortunate in society. God didn't like that. So obviously a living sacrifice is all about offering all that we are and want to be into the hands of God. Simple. Or is it?

I would love it to be simple. But I do find it hard, and it is something I have to remind myself to do on a regular basis. Because it is too easy to say, 'Yes, I'm here, Lord, anything at all you want, I'll go for it.' But to really offer up all of ourselves requires exactly that. All the good and all the bad, all the things that I want to keep control over in my life, all the parts that hurt as well as all the parts that are happy. Being a living sacrifice means giving all of me to God, and only God knows then what he will do with the sacrifice offered.

Jesus,
  it can be hard at times to read your book,
  to hear your voice,
  and then respond to your challenge.

Here is my prayer;
I am all yours, Lord,
I belong to you.
I pray that I can be used for you,
and used by you.
Learn from you,
and give your learning to others.
Change me more into your image every day,
feel more of your heart,
see more of your life
in this special place.
I will try and listen better to your voice,
and look clearer for your touch.
I will try and respond to your call
and watch your work.
Lord, I am yours,
I belong to you.
Now and forever.
Let it be.
Amen.

Day 8 ....

That is why we always pray for you. We ask our God to make you worthy of the life he has called you to live. May he fulfil by his power all your desire for goodness and complete your work of faith. In this way the name of our Lord Jesus will receive glory from you, and you from him, by the grace of our God and of the Lord Jesus Christ.

2 Thessalonians 1:11-12

This sentiment of Paul's is given in almost every writing we have of his in the New Testament. And the sincerity with which he gives these thanks and calls to prayer all seem genuine and honest – not of course suggesting that there have ever been any people who have uttered the words 'I'll pray for you' and don't!

A couple of years ago I was doing a talk in a church where

I had never been before. It's good to feel safe in a place like that, but unfortunately I didn't feel all that comfortable. I just wasn't sure what they expected – what they wanted me to do. It was meant to be a 'youth' service, but with so many 'youth' services nowadays, they are actually all-age services if you are lucky and if you are not they are normal services with four to ten young people added to the congregation.

I did the sermon and tried to talk to the young people, while at the same time making subtle points to the rest of the congregation about how important young people are – especially those who don't go to church anymore. At the door afterwards, there was an elderly lady who looked at me in the way that has a certain knowledge in the eyes (which always scares me because I expect a 'I knew you when you were only a wee boy'). I had never seen her before, but she looked me straight in the eyes and said, 'It's good to meet you. I pray for you every day.' I thanked her – I hope I sounded sincere, because I was. I was very grateful.

That has actually happened a few times, and I hope I leave no one in any doubt as to how highly I value their prayers. For me they are assurance beyond words.

Paul knew the value of prayer – he prayed for others constantly. Those he had met, those he had helped in their work for God, those he had left behind, those he cared about. He lifted them all in prayer to God. And then he told them he was doing it.

Worked for Paul – try it.

Lord,

 there are nearly always things on my mind,
 things that concern me.
 And maybe I don't think of others enough.
 So I want to take a few minutes, Lord,
 and bring a few people before you,
 I'm sure you know them . . .
 Amen.

GO ON ≫→

1. Have you ever felt that people in your church look down on you because of what you wear, what you do, or how you act in church? (Day 1)

2. Is that your problem or theirs? Why?

3. What are the best ways you can think of to be an example?

4. Without backstabbing(!) what kind of things do you feel Christians do today that show they are not putting their mouths where their faith is? (Day 2)

5. How does the fact that the Bible seemingly allows slavery make you feel? What does it teach us all about how we read the Bible?

6. Take some time and write down (just for yourself) those things in the big backpack that you can't seem to let drop off. What are they, how much do they weigh, do you need someone to help you carry the backpack, have you tried to give something to God but then snatched it back? After you have written some things down – get rid of the paper, God knows what you wrote. (Day 3)

7. Name the rules and regulations that are the typical Christian ones? Do you know where to find them in the Bible? Go on and try. (Day 4)

8. Do you know people (maybe you!) who have broken these rules? How did they feel? Did they get to know about grace?

9. What stops people allowing God to fill them with forgiveness and grace?

10. Do you really believe God loves you no matter what? Whatever gets in the way, let it go.

11. Once again Paul is talking about serious root stuff! How often do you hear ministers/youth leaders/ speakers talk about real love? Do you think people get the message? (Day 5)

12. Think of something you and a group of friends could do to actively show someone, or a group of people, that God loves them more than they could imagine? Go and do it.

13. What things are against you? Have you told God about them? (Day 6)

14. Have you ever sat and thought about the power we have on our side – if yes, then do it again, if not, sit quietly and let the King of the universe reassure you.

15. This is a difficult question – is it possible to give all of yourself to all of God all the time? (Day 7)

16. A famous Christian speaker once answered the above question 'no'. But then said we give all we can to all we understand of God as much as we can. What do you think?

17. How much of you belongs to God at the moment?

18. Who do you pray for? Why? (Day 8)

19. Who do you ask to pray for you? Why?

20. Prayer involves action – Paul's certainly did – how are you turning your prayers into action?

KEEP GOING ⟫→

- Love – Song of Solomon 2:10-17; 1 John 4:7-21; Matthew 5:43-48

- Doing it for real – John 12:23-28, 35-36; Matthew 25:31-46; Matthew 5:3-10

- Prayer – 1 Kings 8:22-26, 54-61; 1 Timothy 2:1-4; Luke 11:1-13

- Grace – Romans 11:25-26; Deuteronomy 4:32-38; Galatians 5:1-15